D0843202

21 Ideas for Managers

Charles Handy

21 Ideas for Managers

PRACTICAL WISDOM FOR MANAGING YOUR COMPANY AND YOURSELF

JOSSEY-BASS
A Wiley Company
San Francisco

Published by Jossey-Bass Inc., 350 Sansome Street, San Francisco, California 94104.

Jossey-Bass is a registered trademark of Jossey-Bass Inc., A Wiley Company.

Previously published by BBC Books 1990; Penquin Books 1999.

Manufactured in the United States of America on Lyons Falls Turin Book. This paper is acid-free and 100 percent totally chlorine-free.

Library of Congress Cataloging-in-Publication Data
Handy, Charles B.
21 ideas for managers : practical wisdom for managing your company and yourself / Charles Handy.— 1st ed.
p. cm.
ISBN 0-7879-5219-2
1. Management. 2. Self-management (Psychology) I. Title: Twenty-one ideas for managers. II. Title.
HD31 .H31259 2000
658—dc21

00-008841
FIRST EDITION
HB Printing 10 9 8 7 6 5 4 3 2 1

Contents

ACKNOWLEDGMENTS XI
THE AUTHOR XIII
INTRODUCTION XV
THE CHAPTERS XIX
1 A World of Differences 1
2 The "E" Factor 10
3 The Secret Contract 19
4 The Territorial Itch 27
5 The Inside-Out Donut 36
6 The Johari Window 43
7 The Actor's Roles 51
8 Marathons or Horse Races 58
9 The Self-Fulfilling Prophecy 65
10 The Stroking Formula 74
11 Parents, Adults, and Children 81
12 Power Politics 90
13 Teams and Captains 98
14 Outward and Visible Signs 107
15 Tribes and Their Ways 115
16 Find Your God 126
17 Counting and Costing 141

18 The Customer Is Always There 149
19 Curiosity Made the Cat 158
20 Shamrocks Galore 167
21 Portfolios and Flexi-Lives 176

EPILOGUE 183
INDEX 187

21 Ideas for Managers

Acknowledgments

The images and the anecdotes in this book are new. Most of the theories behind them are long-standing. I am greatly indebted to all who have gone before me and who have educated me in this field by their writings over the years, but most of all I am indebted to my earliest mentors at the Sloan School of Management in the Massachusetts Institute of Technology, Warren Bennis, Ed Schein, Dick Beckhard, and Mason Haire. They set me on a path I am still delighted to tread.

Suzanne Webber of BBC Books gave me the opportunity and, indeed, the courage to write this sort of book, and Nicky Copeland managed to make it much more readable and sensible than it would otherwise have been. I am very grateful to them, and to Gray Jolliffe, who has added humor and art to my prose. My family, as readers will discover, has unwittingly provided some of the case material for the chapters. I am grateful to them for their forbearance. Elizabeth, my wife, has not only typed the manuscript but has been my wise counselor throughout. As with so much of my life, it would not have been half so good without her.

This edition would not have been posssible without the dedicated work of all the people at Jossey-Bass. My thanks go to them all, but particularly to Cedric Crocker, Dawn Kilgore, and Hilary Powers who have helped me to reshape the book for American readers. It has been a delight to work with them.

Acknowledgments

The Author

Charles Handy is, these days, a writer and a broadcaster. He has been an oil executive, an economist, a professor at the London Business School, and a consultant to a wide variety of organizations in both the public and private sectors. He has also been warden of St. George's House in Windsor Castle, a private study center concerned with ethical and social issues, and was for two years chairman of the Royal Society of Arts. He is known to many for his "Thought for the Day" broadcasts on BBC Radio 4's *Today* program.

His first book was *Understanding Organizations,* which was first published in 1976 and is now in its fourth edition. Since then he has published a further ten books, including *Gods of Management, The Age of Unreason, The Empty Raincoat,* and *The Hungry Spirit.* A collection of his "thoughts for the day" is published under the title *Waiting for the Mountain to Move.* His work has focused on the changing shape of work and organizations and what this might mean for our future.

Introduction

Thirty years ago I stood on the steps of the Massachusetts Institute of Technology looking across the Charles River to Boston. I had come to the New World, to the Sloan School of Management at MIT, to discover the secrets of management. I went to MIT because I felt somehow that those secrets were all wrapped up in numbers and technology, in accounting and economics, in statistics and equations and computers—worlds that were all strange and unknown to me then.

By chance that morning, wandering lost and a little lonely down the corridors, I met a member of the faculty called Warren Bennis. Intrigued, I think, by my English accent, he invited me home to meet some friends and colleagues, all of whom taught in the field of "organizational behavior." I had never heard of this subject—I had never thought of organizations *behaving;* indeed, I had never thought much about organizations at all. I had just assumed that they were always there, like the weather, and were also, like the weather, never what they should be.

That meeting in the corridor changed my life. Abandoning my search for numbers, I took up organizations and people instead and, gradually, much of what had mystified me about people and the way they behaved was explained to me. Organizations of all sorts became fascinating places, not boring institutions. The strange behavior of people in groups, in families and in committees, became less strange and more understandable. The way people treat each other, and even themselves, started to make sense once I began to understand a little of what might be going on inside them and between them (something often revealed in the spaces *between* their words).

I understood, and the understanding helped. Sometimes it helped because I was able to see why things were not working as well as they should and so change them. Sometimes, because I could now guess how an individual or a group would react, I was able to work out my approach. Sometimes the understanding just took the surprise out of the situation. If you know that people are bound to quarrel because of the different positions they are in, or because of their different preoccupations, then you are not too disturbed when they do—even if you are unable to prevent it.

The world of people and organizations began to make sense, and since, like most of us, I spend a lot of my time with people or in organizations, I'm sure my life became more sensible, more effective, and certainly more enjoyable. Looking back, I am amazed that the ideas revealed to me during that year in Boston should have been hidden away from me for so long. You would think that these ideas, so simple yet so revealing, would be part of the core curriculum of every school. That, however, is not the case; instead we are left to find out such things by painful experience—by mistakes, lost friends, or family quarrels.

Yet we all need to learn these things because, in one way or another, we all have to get organized if we are going to get anything done, whether it is at home or at work; and getting organized means more than having a datebook and a plan for your week. It means learning how to work with and through other people, because few of us can achieve anything of significance entirely on our own. Getting organized, therefore, starts with understanding why people and organizations behave the way they do. "Know yourself and fear God and you will do well," said the Greeks. They should have added "know other people" because none of us is a hermit or an island—we are all attached to other people. The ideas I found so valuable are like small shafts of light that make so much clear, producing the *Ah-ha effect* ("Ah-ha, of course that explains it").

This book is my personal anthology of twenty-one of these ideas, ideas that may well change the way you see your world and help you to organize it better. Each idea is explained with examples to illustrate it and with a question or two at the end of each chapter to help you apply the idea to your own situation. If you can discuss the idea with the people you work with—or just with friends and family—you will find it easier to work out all that it means for you and, perhaps, for them. I have also thrown in some interludes between the chapters, little stories that I think have a message for most of us.

The book is intended for anybody who has to work with other people and particularly for those with responsibility for others, whether in a work group or a project group, a team or a family. Some of the ideas will strike more of a chord than others; some will make more sense later on when your responsibilities change, or would have been a great help a few years back. The book, therefore, is designed for dipping into, an occasional refreshment for all those who live and work with other people.

> "Well, at least that's one book I won't have to read," said Richard, laughing, when I told him that I was writing a book about getting organized. Richard is our local minister.
>
> "Why not?" I said, just slightly offended.
>
> "Well, it's for managers, isn't it—businessmen, that sort of people?"
>
> "It's not only for them," I said, "it's for everyone who has responsibility for other people or who needs to get things done by other people. And that must include you, Richard," I added.
>
> "Oh, I'm not much good at that sort of thing," he said, "getting people to do things."
>
> "That's the trouble," I replied, "an awful lot of people aren't much good at that sort of thing, but they're running our schools, they're dishing out workers compensation, they're looking after old people, they are raising families as well as running businesses. In fact, come to think of it, almost all of us are managers in some part of our life."
>
> "Should sell a lot of books then," Richard said, laughing again.

Making It Happen is the excellent book by Sir John Harvey-Jones, recounting and reflecting on his days in the Polish chemical company, ICI. The message that I took away from his book was that one makes it happen by making it possible for *others* to make it happen. The director of a play does not appear on stage, even for a bow; directors must produce their effects through other people, tempting though it must sometimes be to do it all by themselves.

This book, therefore, is for all those who want to make it possible for others to make it happen. That, I believe, is the real job of every organizer and of every manager; not to do it all single-handedly. The book is for the supervisor just as much as it is for the regional manager. It is also for the editor of the journal and for the producer of the radio show, for the organizer of the town and the stage manager in the theater, for the foreman in the factory and the PA to the chairman, for the vicar and the schoolteacher, the matron and the hospital's general manager, for the secretary of the boat club and the chairman of the Church Council, for the restaurant manager and for the head chef, for the director of the Institute for Whatever and for its fundraiser, for the local doctor and the local vet, for the manager of the beauty parlor and the farmer down the lane, for every father and every mother. Did I leave you out?

The Chapters

1. A World of Differences

   In which the assumption is made that everyone is intelligent or talented but in a different way. Choose your talent from the list.

2. The "E" Factor

   In which we look at the way people's needs and ambitions change over time and according to the situation. Where were you, and where are you now on the ladder of human needs?

3. The Secret Contract

   In which we examine the unspoken contract each of us makes with everyone we meet but keep so secret that it seldom works. What is in your contract—and do the others know?

4. The Territorial Itch

   In which we look at the ways people stake out their territories in their work and in life, and how crucial this can be. What are your territories and how do you protect them?

5. The Inside-Out Donut

   In which a job, any job, is compared to a donut turned inside-out, with responsibilities mixed with opportunities. Can you draw your donut? Would you like it to be different?

6. The Johari Window

In which one way of thinking about ourselves and other people is revealed and discussed with all its implications. What shape is your window?

7. The Actor's Roles

In which way we see how the parts we are asked to play in life can shape the way we behave and the way people think of us. What parts have you been given? What part would you like?

8. Marathons or Horse Races

In which the different kinds of competitions that happen both in organizations and in life are experienced. Can you devise your own marathon?

9. The Self-Fulfilling Prophecy

In which we examine how so often we live up—or down—to the expectations people have of us. Who expects what from you?

10. The Stroking Formula

In which it is explained why stroking people psychologically usually works better than striking them. Have you had any good strokes lately? Or given any?

11. Parents, Adults, and Children

In which we explore whether we choose to play the adult or the parent or the child in different situations, why we choose each option and what the results can be. Which role do you like playing?

12. Power Politics

In which the different options for influencing people are analyzed. What is your power base?

13. Teams and Captains

In which it is explained why groups are not always teams and why committees never are, and why teams need different sorts of players and a captain. Is your group a team?

14. Outward and Visible Signs

In which we see how the outward signs of organizations and of people say a lot about their inward workings. What do the outward signs say about your organization—and about you?

15. Tribes and Their Ways

In which we explore the very different ways in which different groups of people have chosen to organize things. Choose the organization or tribe to fit your style.

16. Find Your God

In which the different styles of management are given the personality attributes of four Greek gods. Which one best suits you?

17. Counting and Costing

In which it is demonstrated that the cost of anything can be calculated in at least ten different ways. Do you know what the bits of your work really cost?

18. The Customer Is Always There

In which it is argued that, to feel useful, we all need clients and customers, whether we are in business or not. Who is your client?

19. Curiosity Made the Cat

In which the atmosphere which makes successful organizations so avid for learning and discovery is analyzed. The same can also be applied to people. Have you got the appetite?

20. Shamrocks Galore

In which it is forecast that more and more organizations are going to have three leaves like a shamrock, each of a different type of workforce. What part of the shamrock do you work in?

21. Portfolios and Flexi-Lives

In which it is envisaged that for many of us the world of work will be made up of bits and pieces, thus creating the need for everyone to make a personal collection or portfolio. What might go into your portfolio?

1 A World of Differences

Not so long ago I went to see a new program for fourteen- and fifteen-year-olds at a school in the south of England. For two days a week a group of twenty-five students were taken out of normal classes and put into a "special project" program under one teacher. He had organized them into television production teams for the term, giving each group of eight or nine young people the task of researching a topic for a seven-minute public education program, scripting it, and shooting it in the studios of the nearby technical school.

I went along to see the programs being filmed in the studio. Everything was the same as it would have been in real life; the roles played by the students, the tension, the excitement. There was the fifteen-year-old director, the fourteen-year-old behind the camera, the visual aids, and even a rigged-up teleprompter made of sheets of paper held in front of Jimmy, the young presenter. Jimmy, I was told, was the shy boy of the class, the silent one; they, the group, had thought it would be good to give him a go at the presenter role. They were allowed one practice run and then one for real. Jimmy dried up in the middle of the practice in spite of the teleprompter. Robbie, the young director, a tough-looking character, rushed out from the control room and I wondered what would happen. He put his arm around Jimmy, who was white and very quiet.

"That was wonderful, Jimmy, quite super. Now we'll do the whole thing for real and you can go right through it. Any problems?"

"No, thanks, Robbie," said Jimmy, and went on to give a faultless performance next time through. How many managers, I wondered, would have handled that situation half so well?

On the way back to the school I talked with the group.

"What are the rest of the school doing?" I asked. "Why have you been singled out for this exciting project?"

"Oh, the rest, they're in class, studying for exams. They're the clever ones, see? We're the stupid gang, have to be kept out of the way."

That experience finally convinced me that we try to define intelligence in a very narrow way. Research at Harvard University was, that same year, measuring a whole range of different "intelligences," with names like linguistics, logical-mathematical, spatial, and bodily-kinesthetic, and beginning to demonstrate that they could actually be measured and—most important—that they did not necessarily connect with each other. Maybe the Greeks were right when they spoke of different "faculties of the mind."

Forget the technical names. Remember only the key fact that intelligence has many faces that do not necessarily connect with each other. We can be intelligent in more than one sense. My own working list has seven different types of intelligence.

Logical Those who can reason, analyze, and memorize
Spatial Those who can discern patterns in things and create them
Musical Those who can sing, play, or make music of all sorts
Practical Those who can pull a carburetor to bits but might never be able to spell the word or explain how they did it
Physical Those who can get the most from their bodies—the athletes and dancers among us

Intrapersonal Those sensitive people who can see into themselves, the quiet perceptive ones

Interpersonal Those who can make things happen with and through other people

There may be more—communication skills may be a combination of interpersonal and logical or they may be an intelligence in their own right. Problem solving, too, may combine the practical and the spatial or may stand on its own. The precise list is not important. What is important is the possibility, I would say the probability, that everyone is intelligent in some way, if only we could recognize it.

It is the tragedy of much of our schooling that we are led to think that logical intelligence is the only type that matters. Any observation of our friends and colleagues in later life will prove that the other intelligences are at least as important, if not more so. Indeed, all the intelligences in my list are recognized by teachers but too often all except logical intelligence are grouped together as out-of-school activities—in other words, marginal. We should train ourselves to ask not "How intelligent is this person?" but "Which intelligence does this person have most of?"

Many of the chapters in this book will emphasize the importance of having the right mix of people for each situation—of understanding the other person as well as yourself and of treating people as individuals rather than as identical clones. To say that people are all different is, perhaps, a blinding statement of the obvious, but all too often it is forgotten. We assume that everyone will react in the same way, that they are all like us—or sometimes that they are all quite different from us. In the short term, life gets much simpler if we can fit people into boxes: "That's a British football supporter" (and therefore a hooligan); "He's a tax inspector"; "She's a teacher"; even, too often, "She's a woman," or "Well, a man would say that, wouldn't he?" We are all great stereotypers.

> William was at university, clever, talented, and articulate. He dressed fashionably—which meant that he had his hair in a ponytail, wore baggy black trousers, a black sweater, and bulky, shapeless shoes. His parents encouraged him to join them and their guests for dinner one night when he was at home. His look of dismay and contempt when he saw the two gray-suited, cocktail-dressed couples enter the room was obvious, as was

his silent, sulky demeanor during the first half of the evening. He didn't need to say, "What am I doing here with you!"—his face said it for him. However, the conversation warmed up and William joined in. His radical views turned out to be less radical in some ways than those of the guests. He began to warm to their wit and their arguments and they to him. They left late.

"Did you enjoy it?" asked his parents.

"Yes, I did," he said, "once I got behind their appearance."

"That's exactly what they said about you," his parents replied. "They thought you were a delinquent until you started to talk!"

People are different. We each have our own personality and peculiarities but, in some way, we are *all* intelligent. The positive assumption is that everyone can be useful and productive somewhere or somehow, that the differences are useful. The negative assumption is that differences make difficulties and that the more we can flatten down the bumps, smooth the edges, and get people conforming, the easier life will be.

Getting organized used to mean getting rid of differences: nowadays it means using them. This may sound trivial but it matters enormously when it comes to running a business, an office, a school, or even a family.

A *family* of differences means that the children are encouraged to develop their own personalities and talents and not simply follow in the footsteps of their parents. A *school* of differences wants every student to have their own development plan, their own course of studies, and their own personality. A *business* of differences recognizes that talents mature at different ages in different people, that different ways of working suit different groups. The sales department is unlikely to want to mirror the accounts section or vice versa. A whole *society* of differences accepts that there are many kinds of success; that class, or where you were born, is of little relevance to anyone else; that what you wear or how you live is your own concern provided it does not offend your neighbor.

Such a world of differences can easily degenerate into a selfish, egocentric collection of "mind your own business" attitudes. The challenge of getting organized lies in uniting these differences into a common cause. It is easier, without a doubt, to run an organization where people are like robots; where everyone is a number, conditioned to obedience. It is easier but also more dangerous, because it puts all the responsibility for planning the organization, for its strategy and its survival, onto the shoulders of just a few people and, in turn, on the people who have been reared in their image. People grow old and the world changes too fast for that to be a safe strategy. It would be a rash grandfather who tried to predict the right career for his granddaughter. Wise grandparents and wise organizations cultivate the differences and then seek to mix them fruitfully. This is now the secret to getting organized.

> Many years ago I worked for a while in what was then the British colony of Sarawak. Until ten years before it had been literally owned, and administered, by an English family called Brooke. I was impressed, I remember, as I traveled around the country to see how much all the older district commissioners and senior government officials resembled each other. I was told later that the old "Rajah" Brooke had a simple but effective way of recruiting people to serve on his estate before the Second World War. The first prerequisite for appointment was that they had been educated at any of the public schools in the West Country—this was the background of the Brooke family and therefore provided a kind of tribal bonding. Second, they must be over six foot tall (the Dyaks, the native people of Borneo, were small and would, it was thought, be impressed by their taller rulers). If they met these preconditions they were invited to dinner at the Savoy, given two strong drinks before the meal, wine with it, and two strong drinks after it; if they could then maintain a civilized conversation and walk unfalteringly to the door at the end, they got the job. (The Dyaks mixed a powerful drink, which local manners required one to drink and remain unaffected by.)
>
> The story may well be apocryphal in its details, although the officials were indeed all tall, hard-drinking, country-gentleman types when I was there. However, it exemplifies the homogeneous style of organizations in those days: "Get them as much like you as possible, that way you know where you are." This is certainly true—but the organization may not necessarily survive as a result.
>
> Sarawak was ceded to the British government in 1946.

When trying to get organized it helps to know what some of the differences in people may be. The obvious ones—male or female, short or tall, young or old—may not be as important as they used to be or as crucial as the less obvious differences such as the nature of each one's intelligence.

Some of the more interesting but less obvious differences show up in our attitudes to life. For instance, consider the kinds of attitudes outlined in the next three sections.

ORIGINS AND PAWNS

This was a distinction made by a researcher called de Charme in the sixties. *Origins* are people who feel that they are in charge of their own destiny, that what they are doing is of their own free choice. They think carefully about what they want, are aware of their abilities and limitations, and choose their goals accordingly, ruling out those that are too risky or too easy.

Pawns, on the other hand, are people who feel that someone or something is in charge of their fate. They do things because it happened that way, or because they were asked to. Pawns, therefore, do not plan their lives or their actions very deliberately; rather they hope that Lady Luck will smile on them. Often she does. When she does not, they simply write it off and get on with the rest of their life, content to float on the waves of existence.

Organizations of all sorts need both Origins and Pawns; all Chiefs and no Indians makes it very difficult to get organized with everyone trying to take charge. On the other hand, too many Pawns tends to mean no initiatives, no change and therefore no progress. Remember, it is not all bad news being a Pawn; Pawns may be intelligent in any of the different ways listed, they may be very competent and very diligent—they just do not want to take charge of the future.

TYPE A AND TYPE B

This distinction was made by Friedman and Rosenbaum, two other researchers. Type A people, they said, were characterized by "extreme competitiveness, striving for achievement, aggressiveness, haste, impatience, restlessness, hyper-alertness, explosiveness of speech, tenseness of facial musculature and feelings of being under the pressure of time and under the challenge of responsibility." Type B were more laid back in every way, more calm, less enthusiastic, less aggressive—often more pleasant to be with! There have been studies that linked extreme Type A behavior with known risk factors to health such as high blood pressure, high cholesterol, high levels of uric acid, smoking, and lack of fitness. However, it is very difficult for Type A people to become Type B people or vice versa; you are what you are, and organizations, once again, need both.

THE HUMORS

There have been many attempts to categorize personality types, but sometimes I feel that we have not got much beyond the four humors as described by the ancient alchemists. Here are their traditional divisions (with some modern translations):

Melancholic Moody, anxious, rigid, sober, pessimistic, reserved, unsociable, quiet

Choleric Touchy, restless, aggressive, excitable, changeable, impulsive, optimistic, active

Sanguine Sociable, outgoing, talkative, responsive, easygoing, carefree, lively

Phlegmatic Passive, careful, thoughtful, peaceful, controlled, calm, even-tempered

All of us have aspects of each of the four humors in our personality, but the ancients were probably right in thinking that we each have a general tendency toward one.

It is always tempting to try to make the world in your own image; to shape your children or your work group into images of yourself. This is not only hard—it is also usually wrong. Instead, we must learn to delight in the differences, even though it may be hard to watch our children choose different lives and attitudes and values than we chose ourselves. However, there is one thing I know to be true: it is easier to delight in the differences and to make the most of them once you know what they are and how to recognize them.

SOME QUESTIONS FOR THINKING AND TALKING ABOUT

Getting organized requires that you make the best of the differences. Start by classifying yourself and your family or work group according to the list of intelligences given earlier in the chapter.

1. Do you agree with the list? Cross out any you do not recognize. Add any you think should be there. This is *your* list, not anyone else's.
2. Give yourself points on a scale of 1 (low) to 5 (high) on each type of intelligence on the list. Do the same for the other members of your group and add up the totals. They may well add up to roughly the same, demonstrating that most people are equally "intelligent" but in different ways.
3. Look at the work that you do, and the roles that you perform, and do the same with the people you are responsible for at work or at home.
   a. Are you doing the things that you are best fitted for?
   b. Are the people you are responsible for doing what they are best fitted for?
   c. If you or they are not doing what each is best fitted for, what can you do about it?
4. Which of the other ways of describing differences do you find useful? Can you categorize yourself?

"Newly appointed to head my oil company's marketing division in Sarawak, I was twenty-five and eager to prove my capability in my first command. Sarawak is part of Borneo—as big as England but with rivers instead of roads, rivers the native Dyaks use as their highways in canoes powered by outboard motors. My company sold them the petrol for the motors.

I was amazed to discover that all the petrol was delivered in drums up hundreds of miles of river. Very expensive, I reckoned. It would be much cheaper to put in some bulk tanks at the main towns and supply them by petrol tanker.

I got approval from Head Office and installed the tanks at the end of the rainy season, chartered a petrol tanker and filled them up. I had, I have to admit, noticed smiles on the faces of the villagers as the tanks went in but I assumed that that was just wonderment at modern technology. I sat back and waited for the congratulations. Instead, I got an urgent call from the district officer at Kapit, two hundred miles upstream.

'The river has gone down to its dry season level,' he said, 'and your tank is now a hundred feet above the river. No one can get to it. I have a thousand marooned Dyaks here and a riot is pending. How soon can you get some drums up here?'

'Two weeks,' I replied.

'God help us,' he said.

When I next met him I apologized. There had been no riot, but they had run out of beer.

'Next time, ask the natives,' he said. 'They usually know what will work and what won't.'

Ever since then, I have always 'asked the natives.'"

2 The "E" Factor

"What are you going to do about your daughter?" my wife asked. "She's still in bed and it's past midday." I note to myself in passing that it is always "your daughter" when things are troublesome, but only comment aloud that there are clearly no "E" factors in her life this week whereas, if we cared to remember, a month earlier she had been as busy as a bee at college.

"What are these so-called 'E' factors then?" my wife asked, a trifle scornfully.

"They are all the things that trigger energy, excitement, enthusiasm, effort, effervescence, even expenditure. She has clearly decided that there is nothing going on that is worth the effort of getting up for."

"I call it idleness," she said.

So do most of us; or, if not idleness, then we see it as cruel-mindedness or lack of discipline, when people fail to put their "E" into work or their life. When this happens our natural inclination is to appeal to their better natures, "Come on, you can do better than this," and when that fails, to turn to shouts and threats, "If you don't . . . I will—" until, sulkily, they accept that it would be better to comply than get punished. Even then it will be only the minimum of "E"; just enough to pass muster, leaving everyone a loser.

We do not have to look beyond our own lives to know that there are times when the hours go rushing past, when there is no time for meals or even for sleep, when the energy runs high and the adrenaline fills our veins. We also know that there are other times when it is hard to lift an eyelid, let alone get out of bed. It is not simply that sometimes life is full of fun and that at other times it seems all dreary work, for as Noel Coward once observed, "Work is much more fun than fun." However, it does have to be the right sort of work.

What is it, then, that brings out the "E"s? Or, if one is a manager, a teacher, or a parent, how does one get those "E" forces going in someone else? Perhaps it is money.

> I had to work my way through college. I chose to do it by setting up a mini business to print personal stationery and personalized Christmas cards on my small handpress printing machine. The selling and the designing were interesting, the actual printing was not. Two hundred times an hour I had to put a piece of paper or card into the little press, bear down on the handle, release it and take out the card, put it on a pile of finished work with a slip of paper on top to prevent it from smudging—dull, monotonous work but work where no mistakes were tolerated. No one wants a smudged letterhead or one at a slant.
>
> I would work ten hours a day to produce my two thousand cards a day and I would do it for a full month each holiday, forgoing social life or anything other than a brief game of tennis or a walk. I did it for the money, but I did it with effort and energy and even some enthusiasm.

At the time I truly thought that I did it for the money. If I am honest, however, the money was only a means to an end. I realize now, many years later, that I needed the money to stay in college, something I felt was essential to earning a living. Less obvious, however, but probably nearer the truth, I also wanted to prove that I could do it; that I could make money by my own wits and my own efforts and that I did not need to be dependent on anyone for either charity or a job. Here, I have to add that when I eventually did start applying for jobs my would-be employers were much more impressed by my embryo small business than by my degree.

Money, therefore, as a trigger for the "E"s, is deceptive. It is what the money is *for* that matters, not the money itself. When the money is for the basic necessities of life (literally to allow you to bring home the bacon) then it will trigger a degree of effort but little more. No rational human being will do more than is absolutely necessary in order to guarantee that money. Of course, if more effort, more energy, or more enthusiasm produced more money then there would be more bacon, or the opportunity to spend it on more than bacon, on holidays and travel and some of the material comforts of life. That is worth a few more "E"s. Maybe there is also, sometimes, the satisfaction of having done better today than yesterday, or of outperforming your colleagues or rivals. Money then becomes a measure of achievement as well as the means of buying necessities. Entrepreneurs, strangely, don't stop at their first million but go on to their third or fourth even though they will never have the time or the urge to spend it on more houses, cars, or goodies. Money, for them, is the measure of their success.

Money, in other words, is complicated. It is not a motive in itself, it is a clue to other motives.

> John was delivering the ladders the decorators had rented.
>
> "Gosh, it's hot today," he said. "I could do without all these extra orders on a day like this."
>
> "That sounds as if business is good," I commented.
>
> "Yes, unfortunately, it is. Too good!"
>
> "Why do you say that?"
>
> "Well, I get the same miserable pay whether it's good or bad, and I would rather do less work than more work on a day like this. Better to be down by the river with some beer and some friends."
>
> "Suppose they paid you extra for every extra order," I asked. "Would that make a difference?"
>
> "Ah, now you're talking, but they wouldn't, would they?"

If John had been paid extra for extra work he would have been working for the money and what it could buy, but would he also, perhaps subconsciously, have been working to prove how efficient and effective he could be? We will never know. But over the years, different surveys have asked people what they most wanted out of their work; what, in other words, would release the most "E"s in them. The answers have been very consistent, no matter whom you ask, at what level or at what age. One such typical list started like this:

Personal freedom
Respect of colleagues
Learning something new
Challenge
Completing a project
Helping other people

The people in this survey put money twenty-fourth. Perhaps they were kidding us or themselves, but this sort of list has been repeated so many times with so many different groups that it must tell us something. Certainly what it seems to say is that there is more to work than money, and, if we only knew what it was, we would know better how to get my daughter out of bed in the morning, or how to trigger the "E" forces in everyone around us.

> *The thing that excites me most is to see a young boy or girl begin to realize that they are actually very good at something. You can see their eyes begin to shine, their whole personality come alive, a new being is born. You can't buy that sort of thrill.*
>
> —A primary school teacher

> *I remember when we got the Ajaxi contract. We had put in so many hours; we had worried so much, argued and battled together, bullied our suppliers for more resources, staked our reputations, really, on winning that business. When the news came that we had won, people started laughing and crying at the same time, hugging each other—yes, grown men hugging each other in delight. No, there wasn't more money in it for us or anything like that, just the feeling that we had done it. Wonderful!*
>
> —A project manager

Are academics stupid to write articles for journals that never pay a fee? Are doctors mad to go rushing round the world speaking at conferences for nothing? Not at all; they are doing it to enhance their reputations, to improve their standing among their colleagues, and perhaps even to boost their own egos. To pay them is unnecessary because money would not buy what they want: that sense of achievement when we can make a mark on the world—the proof that we are not just human cabbages but are here to make a difference.

> Tom Watson, the founding father of IBM, always tried to give instant recognition for any achievement; for instance, by passing over $500 on the spot to someone who had closed a particularly good deal or come up with a new idea. One day, so the IBM story goes, a young man came to his office to tell him of a spectacular achievement. Beaming with pleasure, Tom Watson searched his pockets and his desk drawer for some form of instant reward. All he could find was a banana. He presented it. It was accepted gracefully and from then on the banana became the symbol of achievement at IBM.

Today, insurance company Allied Dunbar has a glory ladder for its salespeople. They progress through grades named after birds of prey like kestrels and falcons depending on their achievement (the bigger the bird the better, presumably). Building societies sometimes turn their branches into the equivalent of football league divisions, with plaques and prizes for the winners. What these organizations are saying is that you do not need money to release the "E"s, but you do need markers for achievement.

Each of us has some sort of private list of things we want from life. We want the necessities, of course, the food and shelter and comfort that keep us going, but we also want the chance to make a difference and to shine. We also want friendship and the respect of others, the chance to do something useful and worthwhile, and, above all else, we want the chance to be ourselves; to discover all that we are capable of, all that we could be. It may not be possible to prove the statement that by the time we die we have discovered only one-quarter of our talents, but it certainly has the ring of truth about it.

"I want," she said on her twenty-first birthday:

- To be able to pay the electricity bill every quarter without worrying
- To have my own apartment
- To run a little car and keep a little dog
- To go to Greece each year
- To run my own business one day
- To be a mother, but not yet
- To have real friends
- To be of use to someone else
- To be happy

"And your job?" I asked.

"Oh, that," she said, "that's just for the gas bill at the moment, but one day, who knows?"

The more items we have on our private list, the more "E"s we will give out if the task matches the list. The problem is that everyone's list is different. Luckily, however, there is some kind of underlying pattern. There is, for instance, one common priority: we all want to be sure that the necessities are in the basket and for that we need money. Until we have the necessities we will not be interested in luxuries like by-lines and bananas to stimulate our "E"s. Once these are taken care of, however, we all go hunting for our favorite delicacies. For some it will be a chance to create, for some a stab at power, for others fame, or riches, or independence and the freedom to be different. Give me a taste of my chosen delicacy and you can have all my "E." Give me just the bare necessities and you will get only a very barest effort.

Many organizations in the past were, in effect, supermarkets with bare shelves. Only the necessities were on offer. Give people a basic wage, employers felt, and they would and should give you their all. It was, in a sense, a privilege to be in their supermarket at all. The threat of eviction was enough to keep people working, and discipline and good supervision would keep them working hard. It was not only businesses that thought that way—schools, hospitals, and even voluntary organizations assumed that every form of "E" was theirs for the taking just because the individuals had committed themselves to their cause.

They were naive. Everyone needs more inducements than the guarantee of employment to give of their best. The best teachers like their efforts to be noticed, as do the best nurses or, indeed, the best students. We all need our markers; supermarket checkout clerks do not want to be human automatons any more than schoolchildren do, or secretaries. They want to be recognized as individuals, have their ideas listened to, be given responsibility and rewarded for success. They also, of course, want to be assured of the basic necessities. No one is going to be expending energy or effervescence on their work when they have to worry about the bus fare home—the luxuries on the shelves cannot replace the bread and butter. It certainly helps, of course, to be able to believe in what you do, because then you are not just a wage slave, but it is never enough in itself.

> What would happen, I wonder, if we treated schoolboys and schoolgirls the way we treat adult workers? Suppose we gave them money, real money, as a reward for excellence in their work. Would we call this bribery or would we see it, as we do in the adult world, as a performance-related bonus? Middle-class parents do it all the time, of course, with bribes for good exams, ski trips for college entrance, and so on. Perhaps the school could do it, too. Money, after all, is a convenient marker and more acceptable to most than a book on Prize Day.
>
> Suppose schoolchildren were more often put in mixed-age groups with the more senior ones responsible for coaching and supervising their juniors? Would we see this as a bad introduction into the delights of power and privilege for the seniors, or would we see it as we do when we are adults, as the chance to be creative, or encourage others, to get the best out of a group? Which "E"s would the experiment trigger?
>
> Children, at school or not, are only adults with training wheels. They respond in the same way. An exciting school is like any exciting organiza-

> tion—its shelves are filled with opportunities. Every form of "E" is encouraged and rewarded. The necessities are taken care of but everyone knows that there is more to work for. People are individuals, not "hands" or "human resources," and need to be treated as such.

The messages, for me, are clear. Everyone is full of "E," in all its forms. The trick is to release that "E"—the excitement as well as the effort, the enthusiasm as well as the energy. Everyone has a shopping list of what they want from work and life, even if they have not written it down. The more organizations can match these shopping lists, the more they can expect from people. Bread-and-butter offerings will inspire bread-and-butter work. Listen to what people really want and give it to them. No one will be disappointed; organizations that bubble with every type of "E" are fun to be in.

SOME QUESTIONS FOR THINKING AND TALKING ABOUT

Getting organized requires that you release as many of the "E"s as you can in the people around you.

1. Ask a small group of people to discuss these questions:
   a. What would they like *more* of in the organization?
   b. What would they like to see *less* of in the organization?
   c. What would they not like to see changed?
2. Analyze the results:
   1(c) will provide you with a list of some of the good things that effectively buy the basic "E"s of effort.
   1(b) will give you some clues to the forces that block the other "E"s.
   1(a) will give you some clues to the things that could release more "E"s.
3. To release more "E"s, decide these points:
   a. What you can do on your own.
   b. What you could recommend to the organization.

“Paul was driving his tractor with a load of baled straw. I met him on my early morning walk. It was a lovely autumn morning, dew on the grass, a low mist just lifting from the stubble as the sun rose, the first leaves just starting to turn.

‘Up early, Paul,’ I said, by way of conversation.

‘The last of the harvest,’ he said. ‘It’s been a good year.’

‘Will you be getting away for a while now?’ I asked.

‘Don’t suppose so.’

‘Do you never get away?’

‘Only for the odd day, sometimes. I don’t see the sense in it. I love what I do and where I do it. What would I want to go anywhere else for?’

Lucky man, I thought; I wonder how many of us can say that. More should be able to, if organizations got it right.”

3 The Secret Contract

"In sickness and in health . . . for richer, for poorer . . . as long as we both shall live. . . ." The phrases of the traditional Protestant marriage service have an awful completeness about them. It is, when you think about it, a quite formidable public contract that one is signing. I made those vows myself; I signed that contract, but in spite of the magnificent phrases and the solemnity of it all, the contract was still incomplete. It did not specify what our different tasks would be in this new relationship, or what our responsibilities were, or what each was entitled to expect from the other.

My main task, as I saw it, was to bring home the money. Looking back I am amazed that I so readily assumed that this meant I had unquestioned use of the family car to drive to work, leaving my young wife to lug two small kids to school on her bicycle. I had no qualms about leaving home at 7:30 A.M. before the children were up and getting home at 8 P.M. when they were washed, fed, and tucked up in bed. My daughter told me half seriously the other day that she was fourteen before she knew that I existed; I was the man who came to lunch on Sundays. My wife now tells me that those years of her child rearing and my workaholism were the worst of our lives, yet I never even questioned or discussed with her the implicit working contract of our marriage.

People do it differently today. There is, with many couples, a detailed discussion of who does what. Babies are more often a conscious decision undertaken after a lot of thought about the consequences for a changing lifestyle and a readjustment of roles and of expectations. I remember being proud that my wife was a freelance interior design consultant but I still, in my heart of hearts, expected her to look after the children, run the home, and have an evening meal prepared on my return. One day I came back at 8 P.M. to find the breakfast things still on the table, the beds unmade, and the curtains undrawn, and exploded in outrage at such sloppiness. It is the sort of behavior that would mark me down today as an unreconstructed male chauvinist. It was, however, only the outward sign of an unspoken and therefore misunderstood contract between my wife and myself.

These contracts, however, are not confined to the home. They are everywhere. Any relationship, any combination of people involves a match—or, more often, a mismatch—of expectations. Each person has their own unspoken contract in any relationship; not a formal, legal one but a psychological one. The effects, however, are the same as if it were written down and signed; we feel cheated if the other person or persons do not deliver, we look for some "quid" for our "quo" and will hold back on our side if the other side is not forthcoming. The problem with these contracts is that people seldom sit down and hammer them out as they would do a legal one. They make their own assumptions about the different clauses and expect, or just hope, that the other parties have the same assumptions in their version.

> Marina is a graphic designer. She is a good one and has been working for the same company now for eight years. She had, she knew, a track record of success and a string of clients who valued her work. It was therefore an unexpected shock to be informed by an office circular one morning that, in future, all client contact had to be arranged through a newly appointed marketing director, "to main better communication with our customers." "But it's only sensible, Marina, we need someone to be the link person with so many different people doing jobs for the same client,"

> said the senior partner placatingly, when Marina stormed in to complain. "That's not the point," said Marina. "I have always seen it as part of my job to interact directly with my clients, only in that way can I be sure that I am giving them what they want. You cannot take away that right from me without my agreement."
>
> The rights and wrongs of the decision could not be discussed rationally; Marina felt that her (unspoken) contract had been violated. She sulked for the next six months, refusing to cooperate with the new arrangement; her work deteriorated and, in the late autumn of that year, she left the partnership. The senior partner, at first puzzled and then angry, called her uncooperative and selfish and was, finally, pleased to see her go. A talent wasted through misunderstanding.

People are always misperceiving other people's secret contracts. In one factory everybody was asked what was important to them in their work. The foremen were quite sure that the first-level workers would put money on top of the list, followed by "not having to work too hard." The foremen themselves, of course, were more virtuous, putting money and an easy life after things like "a challenging task" or "an opportunity to be creative." In the end, most of the workers put exactly the same things at the top as most of the foremen, with many of them not ranking money at all.

One can just imagine that plant, with the foremen feeling virtuous themselves but believing their men to be both greedy and lazy. The foremen would act on those assumptions without bothering to check them out, creating resentment and anger among people who were actually much more like their bosses than their bosses would give them credit for. Is there some quirk in human nature, I wonder, that makes us think so often that our juniors or our youngers are not as we are, or not as we were at their age or level.

On the other hand, we cannot assume that everyone is exactly like ourselves. Many a senior manager, whose whole being is wrapped up with the job, who is consumed with a passion for the department and has a personal interest in its success, will automatically assume that the same intensity of interest and passion should drive everyone else, be they fledgling executives, secretaries, or drivers. Many of these, however may only be there for the beer, or more prosaically, for the wages and the companionship. Calls for extra effort on behalf of the group will fall on deaf ears unless there is money on the table as well, because for them, in that job, it is only money that matters.

Very crudely one can categorize these implied psychological contracts under one of three "C"s:

- *Coercion:* You are here because you have to be and you do what you are told to do, or else. Prisons, obviously, but also perhaps some schools and even some businesses and government offices behave as if this were the contract.
- *Calculation:* You are here because you have made a straight bargain, so much of something (usually money) in return for effort. More effort, then, deserves more money.
- *Cooperation:* You are here because you want to be here, because you share in the goals of the group and want to contribute. Most organizations like to think this is the contract they have with their employees, but they may be mistaken.

Most people will have different mixes of these three "C"s in the different parts of their lives, but it is not always predictable which "C" will be operating in which situation. There are many families where, despite the parents' intentions, the children feel they are in a coercive contract where the parents have the resources, both physical and financial, to compel them to obey. However, it is important to remember that contracts can change over time—as one rises in the organization, as the children grow up, as one's own needs and priorities change.

> One study I carried out investigated the marriage patterns of a group of executives in their thirties. The individuals were placed, by their responses to a questionnaire, into one of four groups. The "A" group were the "involved" people—they were concerned with achievement and with power, but also with belonging and supporting. The men in this group were in the civil service, in personnel, or in the caring professions. The women all had part-time jobs in teaching or in the professions. Then there was the "B" group, or the "thrusters," who wanted achievement and power above all, the successful business executives, both male and female. There was the "C" group, the "loners" who scored high only on autonomy, being free to do their own thing. And, finally, there was the

"D" group, or "carers," who scored high on belonging and caring but were not too interested in career success. In this rather traditional sample there were no men in this "D" group, only women.

The interesting part, however, came when we joined the partners in their different groups and observed, by talking to them and living with them, how their lives worked as a partnership. These, I may say, were all willing participants and therefore likely to be happy partnerships. The most common combination was a BD marriage, a "thrusting" man married to a "caring" wife. This was an old-fashioned partnership in which the man provided the status and the money and the woman ran the home. They lived, these partners, in traditional homes in the suburbs, with dining rooms, sitting rooms, studies, and kitchens, and they had traditional roles—she cooked, he repaired the house.

They were very different from the AA couple, both "involved," both working, both caring for the children when they could, both cooking and cleaning, in homes with one big common-purpose "living room," sharing friends, responsibilities, and feelings much more than the BD couple.

The BB marriages, two "thrusters" both with big jobs, delegated housework and child care to paid help, ate out a lot on their dual income, and were highly organized but also quite competitive, often in the same career or profession.

This was unlike the last pattern represented in this group, the CC marriage, or partnership, of two "loners" who lived their own lives, shared nothing except the house, ate few meals together and managed their own affairs independently—and expected their children, from an early stage, to do the same.

The first point to note is that all those happy and stable partnerships had different psychological contracts, different sets of expectations of each other. There is no one right marriage contract.

The second point was brought home to me when I began to discuss this research with other people. "You have taken a snapshot in time," they said. "These couples are at different stages of their relationships. We recognize all these different patterns in our own marriages. Many of us started as AA marriages (two involved people) or even BB (two thrusters), then moved to a traditional BD relationship when the family started and one of us, usually the man, had to involve himself heavily in his work. Later, when the children were older, the big question was whether we moved back to an AA relationship with more sharing, or to a CC one in which we both went our own ways."

Happy marriages, I concluded, were ones where both partners knew which pattern they were in and exactly what it involved. You can and should change the psychological contract over time, but you cannot do it independently of each other—both partners have to agree.

These marriage patterns, I now know, are not that different from the kinds of work relationships you find in organizations. It is not too difficult to put the people you know at work into one of the four boxes in terms of what their priorities are: achievement, power, supportiveness, belonging, autonomy, caring, and so on. One can then see how a group of caring "D" people are unlikely to achieve anything on their own but might be excellent as a support group, or that a "B" secretary might not fit well with a "C" boss. The contracts they would secretly make would not be the ones the organization would require. They would be neither happy nor effective.

Psychological contracts are too often secret contracts. We make our own assumptions about what other people expect and, most of the time, we get them wrong. The more we can bring these contracts out into the open, the easier it is to work with people.

> In 1989 a pilot scheme was launched to test the idea of "home–school partnerships." The cornerstone of the idea was an individual contract between school and home specifying what each was expected to do and achieve. It was an attempt to bring out into the open the whole range of unspoken expectations that parents and students have of schools, and that teachers have of their students and the parents.

Many organizations have "Management by Objectives" schemes or some means of setting goals and targets for their people. This is one side of the secret contract and, indeed, an essential one, but the other side is often missing. What is the organization going to do to help, or to give in return if the targets are achieved? All work, after all, is a partnership of some kind. The secret contract made less secret acknowledges this fact, and, by bringing it out into the open, makes it more negotiable. When the contract is left secret, people can feel exploited, manipulated, or ignored and their bosses can become, in their turn, disappointed, angry, or disillusioned.

We need to remember, however, that to be successful the contract has to be accepted by both sides; it cannot be imposed or it will be honored only in letter, not in spirit.

> When I was working in the Far East, part of my duties was to make trading agreements with Chinese agents in each town. After the terms and the discounts had been agreed upon I would pull out the legal document for both parties to sign.
>
> "What do you want that for?" the agent asked.
>
> I looked surprised and answered, "But we have already agreed on it all, this is only the formal, legal bit."
>
> "If it's a true agreement," he replied, "both parties will get what they want from it so neither party will want to break it. Your way, it looks as if you think you have pulled a fast one on me and want to cement it in the law. Only bad deals need lawyers."

SOME QUESTIONS FOR THINKING AND TALKING ABOUT

Getting organized is made much easier if all secret contracts are as open as possible.

1. Start with yourself. Write down answers to these questions:
   a. What do you give to the relationship or to the organization you are in? (For example, time and money, duties and responsibilities, goals and targets.)
   b. What do you get from the relationship or the organization? (For example, money, security, opportunity, companionship.)
   c. What is needed to make the contract more balanced or more exciting?
2. Ask your partner, colleague, or boss to do the same and to compare their list with yours. (It may be easier, initially, to show them your version and ask for their comments.)

3. Use the idea of the contract to discuss with any work group to which you belong the contributions made by, or expected from, each member of the group, and what they feel they get or should get in return.
4. If you want to find out more about the marriage contracts, read my book, *The Age of Unreason* (Harvard Business School Press, 1991), where I have described them more fully.

"I find payslips terribly depressing. The figures start off so hopefully but fade away to almost nothing by the end after all those deductions. For years and years that was money to me, my monthly payslip. Then, one day, I sold a written article. I got a check. It felt great, even though the check was tiny.

For all those years, I reflected, I had been selling my *time*. Now, for the first time, I was selling my *work*. Of course, the work had taken me time to do, and of course the time that I had sold had produced work, usually. Logically there was no difference, psychologically I felt free.

Maybe Marx was right—selling your time, for a wage, is wrong, a form of slavery. Selling your work, for a fee, is OK. What would happen if we all charged fees?"

4 The Territorial Itch

I once made a bet with a friend. He was the personnel manager of a successful advertising agency, one that prided itself on the quality of its creative people. "Our rooms are mirrors of ourselves," I said. "If you let me see the rooms these people work in and the way they have arranged and adorned them, I will tell you what sort of people they are to work with." He smiled disbelievingly but agreed to let me come in early one morning before any of these late-rising creative stars would appear.

It was, I have to say, a very liberal-minded organization in that it maintained a small warehouse of old furniture from which everyone was allowed to pick and choose. It also gave every new occupant of an office a small budget for improvements. They could furnish their room as if it were their own, to suit themselves.

The differences were extraordinary. One office was a designer's craft shop with the drawing-board as the most dominant feature and the walls lined with cork so that a whole mosaic of old ads and other drawings could be pinned to them. There were no chairs, only one stool under the drawing-board, and old coffee mugs proliferated, some of them filled with pens and pencils. The room next door was a replica of a gentleman's study, complete with mahogany desk, sofa, and glass-fronted bookcase, all neat and tidy and leathery. It was not difficult to describe how each inhabitant dressed, how each spent the day, how they spoke and what their jobs were—young creative genius and middle-aged account manager. Nor was it difficult to guess that they had problems in relating to each other, given their different styles and different priorities.

Other differences were more subtle. Some desks faced the door, others had their backs to it. Some rooms were tidy, some a jumble. Some were welcoming to visitors, some positively discouraging, some young and almost frivolous, others middle-aged, some pretentious and some almost so ordinary that their inhabitants seemed to have made no attempt to put their stamp on the space, as if it weren't really theirs. "Are you sure you haven't met these people?" asked my friend. "I don't need to," I replied. "I've met their rooms."

It's obvious, really. We all make little burrows for ourselves wherever we come to rest, and the burrow matches our shape; not physically, of course, but psychologically. It starts in childhood with the drawings above the bed, and then the teenager's room with "Strangers Keep Out" on the door. We each need our territory, even if it's only the kitchen or the garage. We should pity, in fact, all those who have no place to call their own, in the house or in the workplace. Deprived of a corner, they are private only in the lavatory and, in my old school, even those had all the doors removed.

A private territory is important for self-expression; remove it and you are saying, in effect, that self-expression is not wanted, that individuality is a nuisance, that things work better when all share a common space, when all is uniform and all are in step.

There is no doubt that some organizations want it that way. Individual differences can be a nuisance on an assembly line or in a battery of account clerks. Interchangeability, the ability to replace staff immediately at the check-in desk or the cash register, is crucial to efficiency. Standardization means productivity, but standardization means that no one has a private work slot. It is sensible economic logic but it flies in the face of human and, indeed, animal instincts.

> Robert Ardrey is the author of an influential book called *The Territorial Imperative.* In it he argues that a human being "is as much a territorial animal as is a mocking-bird singing in the clear Californian night. . . . The dog barking at you from behind his master's fence acts from a motive indistinguishable from that of his master when the fence was built."
>
> He goes on to describe the stamping grounds of the Uganda kob, an East African deer. "A stamping ground, the breeding arena of a single generation of kob, looks like nothing so much as a series of putting greens conveniently arranged for the benefit of idle guests behind a luxurious resort hotel . . . a stamping ground is not large . . . each little putting green with its close-cropped grass is about fifty feet in diameter and is a territory occupied and defended by a single male. . . . Here, the champion males out of a population of almost a thousand fight, display, and jockey for position. Here, needy females come for consolation.

"Within the arena . . . some properties have greater sexual values than others. . . . The female wants her favors but she wants it at a good address. Since this coincides with the male's sense of value it results in a scheme of natural selection of a remarkable order. Only a superkob lasts long on a central territory. If he leaves it for water and forage he will return to find it occupied and must fight to regain it. He will be continually challenged by the ambitious."

Ardrey comments that the human male, encountering a stamping ground for the first time, cannot fail to identify with what he sees happening.

Territory, however, does not have to mean a room of one's own. Although desirable, in today's city offices that room is becoming an increasingly expensive luxury. Territory can also mean one's job territory, the kind of psychological space your job or your work gives to you. This form of psychological territory is just as important as physical territory and influences our feelings and our actions in much the same way.

Job or no job, we all have our little duties in life. In my youth, I recall, it was trimming the wicks of the oil lamps in our unelectrified rural home. It was not a job I enjoyed, and I certainly did not get paid for it, but it was *my* job. I did not therefore take kindly to my mother doing it for me, unasked, one morning, just because she wanted to get the housework over and done with early that day. She meant it well, no doubt, but to me it was an invasion of my territory and I sulked for twenty-four hours.

You do not have to look very far to see the story of the oil wicks repeated in every organization every day. Somebody somewhere, impatient with the way things are being done, steps in to get it done their way and either forgets to ask permission first or decides not to ask in case permission is not given. Either way, it quickly results in "organizational sulks" that can quickly lead to real conflict.

The demarcation disputes that were such a feature of industrial relations in the sixties and seventies were territorial arguments, institutionalized. However, do not imagine that now that more employers have negotiated flexible work agreements the issue of territory has disappeared—it has only gone from the negotiating table. Territory, real or imagined, is a most precious possession, not to be yielded up easily, not to be invaded without offense.

> As deputy head, Margaret was responsible for the school timetable. "I am the scheduler around here," as she put it—the only one who had all the information to put the complex mix of rooms and students and staff together in the seven hours that made up the school day. Once created, the ordered sequence of classes was as difficult to change as an official railway timetable. One change only set off another, as Margaret repeatedly said, it would never end, so better not allow any changes at all.
>
> John and Angela, however, had a problem. They both needed some double periods in Room 5 where Margaret had only allowed for singles. They made an informal swap agreement whereby they gave each other two periods and took two periods back, thus allowing them to put their four singles together into two doubles. No one else was affected. No one else was concerned. No need, as they saw it, to tell anyone. They just did it.
>
> Margaret, of course, found out. A sick child triggered a visit by Margaret to the classroom where John, not Angela, was presiding. Inquisitions, denunciations, and fury followed. In vain did John and Angela protest that this was a purely local arrangement. They had no authority, said Margaret, it was a violation of the rules. It must be undone. No appeal was to be allowed.

It was, of course, crazy, the principal agreed, but they had trampled on Margaret's territory. Fences must be repaired, the trespassers must apologize, Margaret must be given back her rights. This done, and anxious to show that she was not beyond reason, Margaret soon came up with an even better schedule that gave John and Angela all they wanted. But two weeks had been consumed in resentment, distrust, backbiting, and argument. Trespassing is a violation even when it is sensible.

People protect their work territories in all sorts of ways. Most obviously, they use physical barriers as markers—watch the open-plan office disintegrate into the little putting greens of the Uganda kob, marked out by potted plants, filing cabinets, screens, and, eventually, the soundproof wall and the outer office with secretary standing guard. More subtly, the territory is protected by information. If I, and only I, have all the information then no one else can properly act without my agreement. If territory protection is your main concern then make sure that all information comes to you but that not all information is distributed.

Good managers, of course, keep "open house." No drawers are closed, no doors are locked, all books are on display. That kind of philosophy, however, requires more self-confidence than one might expect, and more trust in one's colleagues. Cliques and mafias might form, they might discover that you were unnecessary, they might end up knowing more than you. It is all too tempting to reassert the authority of the landlord, to close the doors, to keep one locked cabinet, to admit by invitation only.

Few of us keep a completely open house. We like people to remember that it is *our* house, that in the end the work is *our* responsibility, for which we will get the credit or the blame. Conversely, we need to remember that when we enter other people's job territories, however welcoming they are, we should enter by invitation, should behave circumspectly, and should remember who is the host. To forget those simple rules of courtesy is to invite closed doors and locked cabinets and frosty smiles.

Groups have their own ways of fencing off their territories. In some organizations there are still separate dining rooms for separate grades. I remember how, in the middle of a meeting in one such stratified company, we broke for lunch. I and another went down to the cafeteria. The rest went up to an executive dining-room on the twenty-third floor. Waiting by the elevator it was clear who were the insiders and who the outsiders. It was also clear where and by whom the real decisions would be taken.

Groups also have more informal ways: they create their own language and their own culture (have you ever been a newcomer in a sailing club?); they have their little rituals (Friday evening at the local bar); they pepper their communications with initials which can be known only to the initiated (copies to MKC, DJF, P Fin, and JFR); they hug information to themselves (no, there are no minutes of our Monday morning gatherings). It can be as hard to break into some groups as it is to break into a tightly locked football huddle.

Groups need their territories. It is one way in which they define themselves as a group. But if those territories are too well protected, the group becomes an island, cut off from the rest of the organization. Like so much in management, there has to be a compromise. It helps if one can give the group their own physical territory or club room; they then will need to use fewer of the more psychological defensive measures as a substitute for a place of their own. They must, however, be encouraged to welcome others into their club room. Schoolchildren, deprived of such a room and forced to scurry from one teacher's classroom to another, soon form gangs to give themselves the protection of another form of territory. Indeed, why is it that in secondary schools it is the teachers who often stake a claim to the classroom, not class groups? Again, it is perhaps as much for territorial security as for convenience.

Reorganization inevitably means a redistribution of territory. This is perhaps the reason why it is so disliked by so many and also, ironically, why it is so frequently the favorite device of those at the top for loosening up the organization. Victorious states, after winning the war, almost invariably redraw the frontiers and redistribute the land. Any revolution almost inevitably leads to land reform. It is no different in organizations and the reactions are the same—desperate resistance from the dispossessed, followed by sullen resignation and the silent packing of belongings. Triumphant possession by the newcomers is followed by the natural desire to stamp their own mark on the new property, just as new owners almost always redo the kitchen of their new home, even if it is already immaculate.

Territory, after all, is security and territory is power. It is hard to give it up. Even on promotion, the urge to cling to the familiar can be stronger than the pull of the new arena.

> Richard had been promoted. The organization had grown so fast that a new layer had had to be created in head office. Richard was now supervisor of all the regions whereas before he had been regional coordinator for New York and the Southeast.
>
> What it actually meant was that another desk had been squeezed into the corner of the big room where Richard had always worked. He moved just ten yards from his old desk to a new and slightly bigger one. He looked straight across at the back of his old chair where Barbara now sat—a new promotion. It was cramped and inconvenient, but Richard was no stickler for protocol, and anyway he expected to be very busy, out and about, responding to the requests and needs of all the regions. Strangely, however, there weren't any. Instead there was a sense of silent antagonism from his old regional colleagues who used to report, like him, to the director but now had to answer to him. It wasn't intended as any sort of personal affront, but it began to feel like it to Richard.
>
> Frustrated and suffering for a change from too little to do instead of too much, Richard turned his mind back to his old haunts where Barbara, his replacement, obviously had a lot of learning to do. "Let me deal with that," Richard would say, after hearing Barbara on the phone, or "I would be careful there," or "Would you like the background on that, Barbara?"
>
> It was even more hurtful to be told, politely, by Barbara, "No, thanks, Richard. I'll deal with this in my own way." After all, it used to be his desk, they used to be his problems, his babies. It felt like that. It can be awful to lose your territory and not know where to find the new one.

Territory is something we take too much for granted and therefore pay too little heed to. Ask any organization what its chief problem is; people will reply, nine times out of ten, "communications." Most of the time the poor communications are but a symptom of some territorial problem or dispute. Ask any family why there are problems—"because we don't understand each other." Often, that is another way of saying that some of us do not respect the right of others to have their own territory, to be free to do their thing in their own way.

Thinking territorially explains a lot about people. It will not always tell you what to do but it may tell you what not to do. Sometimes that is just as useful.

SOME QUESTIONS FOR THINKING AND TALKING ABOUT

Getting organized requires one to think territorially, both physically and psychologically. Use "territory" as a metaphor in your discussions with the group. It is a useful way of describing problems that can otherwise become unduly personalized.

1. Do you have a physical territory? How would you like to improve it? Is it welcoming to outsiders or forbidding?
2. What is your psychological territory—your area of responsibility? Is it well recognized by others? Can you define it more clearly?
3. Discuss with your work-group their territories, both physical and psychological. Are they happy with them? Suggest any improvements.
4. Are there clear territorial rules, such as who can visit or inspect one's territory without invitation? Is permission needed? What forms of control are legitimate "landlord's prerogatives" and what are not? Discuss what the ground rules are and should be.

"The list of credits on the television documentary last night was very long. I calculated that it took up over two minutes of screen time. That, I imagine, is a lot of money. Why do they do it? I mean, I am not interested in or influenced by the fact that Doreen Ismael is the assistant wardrobe keeper. Yes, the names of the director and possibly the cameraman and narrator were important. I could remember them—it is useful information. But the rest . . . ?

'You've got it wrong,' a television friend who was with me said. 'You may not need to know who they are, but they need to tell you who they are. This is their way of signing their work. And I can tell you,' he added, 'if we get those names wrong by even one letter there's hell to pay.'

Why can't we all sign our work in some way?"

5 The Inside-Out Donut

"Well, that's done then," said the electrician, beginning to put his tools away. "Thank you," I said. Then I noticed that a white wire lay obtrusively along the side of one of the roof beams. "Does that wire have to be showing?" I said. "It looks ugly." "Well," he said, looking defensive, "it could be traced into the wall, but you didn't ask me to make it invisible, did you? And anyway, I've got to be off now, so if you want it changed it will be another job," he added, backing out of the door as he spoke. I lived with that white wire for years, thinking every evening, "Why do I have to spell out everything to these idiots? Can't they ever use their initiative?"

A job is a job is a job, my boss used to tell me. He would be wrong today. A job is now, to a large extent, what you make it. It is like a donut turned inside-out! Let me explain.

For the purposes of getting organized you need to turn the donut inside-out in your mind, so that the hole is filled in and the empty space is on the outside—if you can conceive of that. It looks like this:

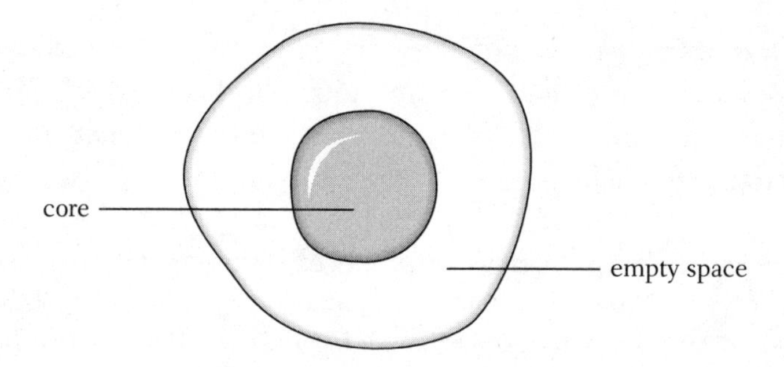

Think of it as a fried egg if you prefer; to me the Inside-Out Donut Theory of Management just sounds more intriguing than the Fried Egg Theory, but everyone to his or her taste!

The theory goes like this: in all our jobs or roles there is a set of things that, if we do not do, we have failed. These things may be written down in a contract or they may be in an official job description in your desk drawer; if you work in a classy organization you may have a set of targets or objectives, or it may be a clutch of things you know you must do without anyone having to remind you, such as washing, dressing, and feeding the children, and getting them to school.

The door's still locked at ten o'clock and someone has overslept, the food unordered for the restaurant and someone clearly has failed, no gate to receive the incoming aircraft, no editorial for tomorrow's paper—the signs of failure can be trivial and obvious or crucial and less immediate, such as when top management fails to invest in some new technology and the competition leaves the firm in the dust.

The things you must do or you are judged to have failed represent the solid core of the inside-out donut, the yolk of the egg. Life, however, is unfair. There is a catch-22. Even if you do all that is asked of you, you have not succeeded. More is expected. You are meant to fill up the whole of the donut, the white of the egg as well as the yolk. The trouble is, no one could tell you in advance what is expected of you in that empty space because, if they knew, they would have put it in the list of things in the core. This space is the truly empty space in the donut, the space where you are meant to use your own initiative to improve on the core, to expand the necessary tasks so they fill the donut right to its invisible boundaries.

In times past it was not like that. People were expected to do what they were asked to do and no more. "Push this handle one hundred and fifty times a minute." "Fill in these forms like this—no variations allowed." "Keep to the timetable."

> Some people have narrow minds. Once, working in the oil industry in the Far East, I had responsibility for a number of oil storage depots. There were clerks in each, responsible for logging the inflows and outflows every day and checking the results against the dipstick readings in the tanks. They entered all their numbers in the official log book. They were uniformly good workers, meticulous in their timekeeping, neat and accurate in their numbering. One day, however, visiting an outlying depot, I looked at the log book. Up-to-date and tidy, I saw, but then I noticed that there was a steadily growing discrepancy between the quantity that should have been in the tanks, if you subtracted what went out from what went in, and the stock that was actually there. Something was leaking, or someone was stealing.
>
> "How long has this difference been noticeable?"
>
> "Twenty days," said the clerk.
>
> "Why haven't you done anything about it?" I asked angrily.
>
> "My job is to keep the figures, sir. No one told me I had to interpret them as well."
>
> I know accountants like that too!

In the past it was, in fact, inconvenient if people did exceed their responsibilities. Organizations were intended to run like clockwork and were therefore designed like clocks, with every part in its place, and a well-defined place for each part. Families were like that too, and so were school classrooms and hospitals (some still are).

It worked tolerably well, perhaps, in a world where little changed. The organization could assume that what worked well yesterday or last year would work well tomorrow. More important, the people at the top knew what was going on—or should be going on—in every little area. That kept things under control. It was said that the French Minister for

Education used to be able to look at his watch and his calendar and know what every child in every school in France was studying—so well organized was it all. Many managers in the past would have aspired to the same kind of precision. So would teachers, ward sisters, and army drill sergeants; it was a world where all the donuts were pre-filled with instructions.

> I cannot now, in middle age, remember much of what I learnt at school. Bits of memorized poetry, some multiplication tables, a snatch or two of jumbled history, and some strange place names like Hindu Kush or Montevideo that I would be hard put to find on a map, let alone visit. One thing, however, I did learn—too well! That was that every problem in life had already been solved somewhere, by someone. The answer was around already; in the teacher's notes, in the back of the textbook, in the Mastermind answer sheet. The trick, I discovered, was to find out who had the answer, then the problem was solved. It took me many years to come to terms with the fact that most problems are, in their own way, new problems which we have to muddle through and to which we must find a new solution. Old answers can help, perhaps, but old answers are not necessarily the answer to new problems. My schooling prepared me for a world of donuts that were all preprogrammed by older and wiser heads. I soon found that most of my jobs and roles in life had an awful lot of empty space. Most alarming of all was becoming a parent. No books or lessons had prepared me for this frightening responsibility; one in which failure was all too obvious, success a long way off and, anyway, hard to define; a role in which there seemed to be endless new questions and no one to answer them except my wife and myself.

Our donuts today have a lot more space outside the core. The white of the egg is much bigger than the yolk. This is partly because everyone wants room to exercise a little more choice, a little more control over their own time and work. It is also because people are better educated nowadays and thought to be more capable by their own superiors. Most of all, however, it is because the world is neither so predictable nor so controllable—things can no longer be totally predicted in advance and the appropriate instructions issued. Of course, the checkout assistant at the supermarket has a job full of instructions and a bell to press when the instructions run out, but even in that drilled and disciplined work there has to be room for the unexpected—the batty customer, the malfunctioning computer, the angry shopper—situations where no preprogramming can help, where the individual assistant has to fall back on personal initiative and common sense. To say, "There is nothing, madam, in my manual about this"—that is not going to be good enough.

Larger donuts mean, in effect, more responsible jobs with more competent people in them. These people, inevitably and rightly, cost more money, but fewer of them are needed and, most crucially, fewer others are needed to tell them what to do and then to check that they have done it. It used to be called "job enlargement"—but too often job enlargement only meant more of the same for more money. Larger donuts with more empty space mean different jobs, jobs with room for new decisions, for initiative, for discretion, for choice between alternatives.

That is why organizations everywhere are getting "flatter," with fewer levels of authority and more people reporting to the one above. They are talking, in Japan, of one foreman supervising a hundred people. Someone can do that only if they all look after themselves most of the time, can use their own judgment, and are both able and allowed to take initiative—if, in other words, their job donuts are big and spacious. It will be the same in the classroom; teachers have, and have to have, increasing autonomy. The new principles of education push that even further by asking the students, too, to think for themselves, to use their own initiative to fill up their donuts instead of expecting the teacher to tell them what to do all the time. Salespeople, maintenance crews, plumbers and electricians, cab drivers and airline pilots, they all have rules to keep and systems to obey—but they are also expected to go beyond the systems when the unexpected arises or an opportunity occurs.

> We asked John (that electrician again) to fix a security light on our garage wall, one of those lights with a sensor on it so that it lights up when you walk by it. "Sure," he said, "I can do that whenever you want." Later that week we were speaking to another electrician, Maurice. "Those security lights don't deserve their name these days," he said. "Every burglar knows about them, they just give him more light to do his work, they don't scare him off. I'll tell you what, though, I could attach the sensor to a light inside the house, by a bedroom window; that way it will look to any

intruder as if they had woken up someone inside. Now that really might scare them off."

John would not have failed if he had done what we had asked, but he would have kept to the core of his donut. Maurice was really filling up the space in his. We'll go back to him, not John, when we need more work done.

Managing people with large donuts can be worrying—you cannot know what they are doing all the time. As with the enterprising child, you want to encourage them to be independent, but what if they get it wrong? To manage their donuts you must specify the core with great care, then at least you know that the essential tasks will be understood and the key rules kept; the outside boundaries of the donut must also be well understood: "Do not go outside here," "Do not spend more than $x," "Do not act without the agreement of the finance department," and more such boundary-setting instructions. More than that, however, is needed. The individual needs to be quite clear what the purpose of the work is. If he or she is to exercise initiative, and if that initiative is going to be useful, then everyone must agree on what will count as an improvement. If students use their initiative and discretion to play truant instead of researching their project, then the large-donut philosophy will be a mistake. They need to be committed to that project, the teacher needs to be able to trust them, and someone has to make sure that they have the competence to do the research that is needed. It is no good having lots of opportunity if you don't have the training to make use of it.

Shared commitment, trust, and training—the prerequisites of good donut management and of *any* good organization. Easy to say, difficult to achieve. Donut thinking, after all, is as old as the hills; there is even the parable of the talents in the Bible where the father distributes money to his sons, whereupon one hides it away and returns it intact, feeling proud that he has done his duty, but the other invests it and returns it multiplied—a donut filled beyond the core. We should be glad. Donuts with lots of space outside the core mean more opportunities for us to contribute our special talents. No longer cogs in a clock, we are individuals with a difference to make.

SOME QUESTIONS FOR THINKING AND TALKING ABOUT

Getting organized requires some deliberate donut thinking.

1. Start with your own job, or one of them.
   a. Write down what you think is the core, what you *have* to do.
   b. Write down the limits of your discretion or authority, if there are any (entrepreneurs know no limits).
   c. Write down your understanding of what would be recognized as success in your work, give a few examples.
2. Show this list to your partner or boss.
   Do they agree? Work out with them a shared definition of success, a way of measuring it, and a program of training to help you fill up an even bigger donut.
3. Get your subordinates to do the same exercise and discuss it with you.

"It had been a wonderful concert. The cathedral choir had been at their magnificent best. We had felt proud to see our nine-year-old chorister son singing that wonderful music in such good company. When we collected him from the side door at the end of the concert, however, his face was a study in misery and a tear trickled down one cheek.

'What's happened?' we asked anxiously.

'Mr. Robinson looked at me in the last chorus,' he said, biting back more tears.

'That doesn't sound so dreadful. What sort of look?'

'An angry one. I sang the wrong note.'

'I didn't hear it.'

'No, you wouldn't, but he did, I did, we did. I let them down.'

No wonder, I thought, that it is such a good choir. They call it 'zero defects' in industry, I reflected, the choir just calls it 'in tune.' You are either in tune or you aren't. That's quality. And he does it all with a look!"

6 The Johari Window

It was the first week of a management education program. I was the only non-American member of the group and it was also my first week in the United States. I was nervous, apprehensive, and on my best behavior. I therefore concealed my surprise and alarm when the course organizers announced that the first week of the program would take the form of a completely unstructured group meeting—what they call a "T group" or a "Training Group."

The idea was to put twelve of us in a room for five days with no agenda, no leader, no timetable, and leave us to our own resources. There was, it is true, a member of the staff there to see that we did not physically attack each other or break down, but essentially the idea was that we would reveal more of our true selves to each other if there were no roles to hide behind, no jobs to do, no deadlines to meet.

I had never been in a group like that before. Why, even at a social event there is a host, a timetable of sorts, and an understood list of things to talk about. You know what you are supposed to do and when you are supposed to leave. Not in this group! Still, I was the outsider, I would keep quiet and watch what they got up to.

They got angry. This was not what they had all paid good money for, they said. "What are we supposed to do?" they asked the staff member. "Whatever you like," she said. "This is all nonsense," one man said. "If we've got to sit here let's at least do something useful like make out a list of books we will need for the course." "That's silly," said another. "I think we should form an investment club to play the stock market." They were off! Arguing about the task, forming little groups, sticking their oar in, challenging the leader—*behaving,* in other words, and giving each other all sorts of first impressions.

At five o'clock someone suggested that we check out those first impressions. "Let's play a sort of consequences," he said. "Put your name at the top of a piece of paper and pass it round the room. We will each put a word or a phrase to describe how we see you and fold the paper over before passing it on. When all the papers have gone round, we will each unfold our own and will find eleven words describing how we come across to the group."

Well, I had nothing to lose. I had said nothing, contributed nothing. I would get back an empty sheet of paper. But I did not—it had the full complement of eleven comments, and I did not like any of them: "Snob;" "Old School Tie," "Patronizing," "Stand-offish," "Stuck-up," "Superior," "Unapproachable," were just some. I suddenly realized that they had dumped all their stereotypes of the British onto me. I jumped to my feet, stung at last into speech. I read out the list, red-faced and furious, "And I'm not even British," I said. "I'm Irish." They laughed. I forgave them, I was in, I had made my mark and this time it was me speaking, not a silent stereotype.

I realized then that even if we do not speak we are still giving off messages. Someone once said that as soon as an Englishman came into a room and said "Hello," he could tell what sort of house he came from, what sort of school he went to, which newspaper he read, and what party he voted for, just from the way he dressed, his bearing, and his accent. This man might be wrong in his assessment, of course, but he will still make it, and first impressions have a way of lasting. After my experience I realized that unless I gave a new acquaintance or a new group some

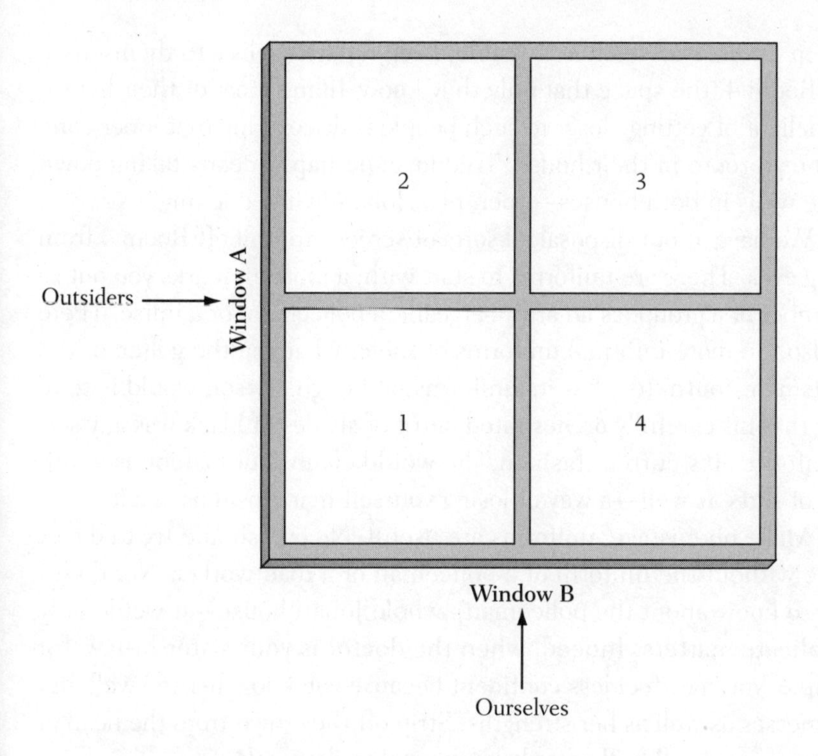

clues to the real me, they would jump to their own conclusions, whether I spoke or not.

It was then that I heard about the Johari Window. Johari is not some Egyptian sage but an amalgam of Joe and Harry—two teachers who came up with a neat diagram to explain what is going on. They called it a window, but I think of it as a house with two windows and two walls:

The house represents us, each of us. Anyone can look in through Window A, but only we can see through Window B. Room 1, then, is common knowledge; it is the part of ourselves that we see and others see. But there are three other rooms. There is Room 2, the aspect that others see but we are not aware of, and there is Room 4, our private space, which we know but keep from others because we are shy or just private. Finally there is the mysterious Room 3, the unconscious or subconscious bit of us that is seen by neither ourselves nor outsiders.

Some people have no guile, no secret selves—what you see is what they are. Room 1, in other words, fills most of their house. Others prefer to keep Room 1 as small as possible, keeping themselves to themselves, with Room 4, the space that only they know, filling most of their house. The delight of getting closer to such people is discovering that inner core, the fourth room in their house. True love, perhaps, means taking down all the walls in both houses—open-plan Johari living, one might say.

We have at our disposal all sorts of screens to wall off Room 4 from prying eyes. There are uniforms to start with; a uniform marks you out as a member of a group, as an army sergeant, a policeman, or a nurse. There are also the more informal uniforms of the city banker, the golfer, or the yachtsman. Youth, too, has its uniforms, although my son would hate to think that his carefully orchestrated outfit of shades of black was any sort of uniform. "It's current fashion," he would claim, but fashion is a uniform of sorts as well—a way of losing yourself in a crowd or in a job.

Make no mistake, uniforms are useful. No one should try to direct traffic without the uniform of a policeman or a road worker. Nor do we need to know about the policeman's whole Johari house—it would only complicate matters. Indeed, when the doctor is your sister-in-law, for example, you may feel less confident because you know her too well, her weaknesses as well as her strengths. Strip off the crown from the head of a king and you will find an ordinary mortal underneath.

If uniforms run out, we can then use conventions or rituals as screens. Polite society used to forbid the discussion of religion, politics, or sex at the dinner table because these subjects tended to promote discord as people revealed more of their private feelings; safer by far to keep to the weather, the Russians, or the state of the championship (football, golf, or racing, depending on the company). By keeping to the conventions it is possible to get through an entire party without saying anything about oneself or even starting a sentence with "I." In this way we keep the screen firmly in place.

All of us live in Johari houses. The first thing we need to think about is whether we want all the rooms to be the same. Do we want to be different people in public and in private, do we want to be a slob at home and a well-dressed executive at work, or even vice versa? There is no right and no wrong. The house is *our* house, it is us, we can live as we please—but we must face up to the consequences.

> My teenage children and their friends make it a point of principle not to dress as their parents would have them dress on some more formal occasions. "Your grandmother is coming, so will you please do your hair and, for once, put on a decent shirt instead of that old T-shirt." It leads to many arguments. We accuse them of laziness, of lack of consideration for their elders, of perversity and selfishness. They charge us with hypocrisy, wondering why we should want them to present an image of themselves that is false.
>
> In Johari language the argument is about whether Room 2 (the public room) can or should be different from Room 4 (the private room). Youthful idealism would have the whole house open-plan with no walls at all. Elderly realism (or cynicism) says that people do not always want the whole truth; that life is easier when we use uniforms or conventions to screen off the private bits of us. Both views are right, but the argument would be less ferocious if it were conducted in Johari language rather than as a battle of principles.

Common sense suggests that life would be easier all round if Room 1 were by far the biggest room in the house; if our public face and our private face were both the same, if the way people saw us and the way we saw ourselves coincided exactly. If that is what we want, however, then we must be prepared to listen to what people tell us about ourselves and we must be honest in telling people what we really feel about things. We must open the doors to Rooms 2 and 4.

That is not always easy. Large organizations, these days, have six-monthly or annual appraisals or reviews. The idea is to have an open and frank discussion about past performance and future goals between a boss and a subordinate. It is well meant, but hard to do. We are naturally defensive and only want to hear the comments that agree with our view of ourselves or our work. In other words, we don't want to go into Room 2, their view of us, and we don't want to open the door into Room 4, our private room. We will only do this for those we love and who we know love us, and love is not the sort of word you meet with much in organizations.

Perhaps it should be; the sort of love, that is, that one feels for one's children or for a very old friend—"unconditional positive regard" they call it in the jargon, the sort of feeling that says, "Whatever you do, I will still be on your side. I may hate the sin, but will still love the sinner—nothing is too awful for me to forgive if you are my child, even though I may punish you for it at the time." Only when we feel that way about other people will they be completely honest with us, and only then can we be completely honest with them and know that they will value us even more, not less, because of it. "I can forgive anything you get up to," I told my children, "except a lie, because that means you don't trust me to understand and forgive."

Without that kind of trust or love we bolt the doors between the rooms and then it is very hard indeed to know who the other person really is. Some people prefer it that way, many organizations do. In those organizations they do not really want to know too much about you. "Please leave your feelings at home, along with your domestic worries." They want you to do the job, collect your pay, and not to speak unless you are spoken to. They want cogs for a well-designed machine—"role occupants," not whole people, "hands," not humans. It keeps things simpler, but they miss out on all the other bits of their people; Rooms 1 and 2 are, in that world, very small indeed, because most of the person is shut up in Rooms 3 and 4.

> I once worked for a large international company. Every day I went in at 8:50 A.M. to a large room I shared with three other people, and we all left at 5:20 P.M. sharp, always, the job done for the day. There was a large oak door to the room and screwed into the outside of that door was a large metal plate embossed with the name of the department, Regional Marketing Coordination—Europe, and below this imposing title there were four slots for plastic slips with four names. Mine was the bottom one. They could be very easily removed and replaced with other slips and, indeed, they sometimes were; the job went on just the same. Suddenly I knew what it was to be a "temporary role occupant," and instinctively I put very little of myself into that office, into my Room 1.

Room 3, our unknown self, is always a bit of a mystery. There lie bits of our past and bits of our inheritance. We should not block them off because they can explode unexpectedly into the other rooms of our life. There are techniques such as psychoanalysis that specialize in the exploration of Room 3, but for most of us it is enough to be aware that it exists, that we are not people without a history, without deep-seated hopes and fears and prejudices, talents and weaknesses.

The Johari Window, or house as I prefer to think of it, is a constant reminder to us to keep the doors open between the different rooms. It should also be a reminder to a manager that the windows only open into half of the house of any personality, a half that may be unnecessarily small. It can never be sensible to work or to live with only half of a person. But the doors to the back rooms, Rooms 3 and 4, cannot be forced, they can only be opened by the person who lives there when the mood is right—a mood of trust and confidence, which always takes time to build.

SOME QUESTIONS FOR THINKING AND TALKING ABOUT

Getting organized means being clear about what is in each room of your Johari house, and in the houses of your colleagues. Only then will you be sure that you, and anyone else, are actually dealing with the same person.

1. Think about your abilities and skills.
   a. List for yourself all the things you think you are good at, with some examples.
   b. List for yourself the things you think you could be good at, given a chance.
   c. Find fifteen friends or colleagues. Ask each of them to tell you one thing you are good at, in their view. Compare their list and yours. Where they overlap is Room 1. The bits they list but you do not are Room 2. Your extras are Room 4.
2. Now, if this was not too embarrassing, do the same exercise with your bad points, but make sure that you choose friends who will tell you the truth. You now have your Johari Window and are in a position to decide whether you want to open any doors between the rooms, or close some off.
3. Do the same with your family, work-group, or team, only this time get everyone to make lists for one another.

"'What do you do?' I asked him.

It was a lovely day. We had wandered down to the pub. We had got to talking. He was alone but with a dog, as was I. The dogs had introduced themselves. We could hardly do less.

'Nothing really,' he said.

'You mean you've retired?' I asked. He didn't look that old, but I didn't want to say 'unemployed.'

'Oh, no—I'm still alive and living. Why do you want to know?'

'I'm sorry, I didn't mean to be nosy. I suppose I wanted to get some sort of fix on you.'

'I'll tell you where I live and what I believe—will that do?' It did very well, actually, and I never did discover what he did. That evening, a lady sitting beside me at a dinner asked me what I did.

'I'm a professor of management,' I said.

'Oh,' she said, and that was the end of that conversation.

Next time I'll take a lesson from my friend in the pub. I won't tell people what I do. Why is it, I wondered, that so often we assume that if we know someone's job we know enough about them?"

7 The Actor's Roles

"I don't see how you can call yourself shy," she said. "You stand up there in front of a hundred people, holding them fascinated, telling stories, totally in command, no streak of nervousness, no sign of fright—I couldn't do that—and yet you say you're shy in front of strangers."

"Ah, but I'm in a role," I said. "I am licensed to perform. Put me down, however, in a group where no one knows who I am, where I am just a rather ordinary face and body, and I will say nothing. No one has given me a part and I find it hard to break in. When I do, there is a moment's silence and the conversation resumes as if I had not spoken—it's the 'plop' effect, as when a pebble drops into a pond and then sinks silently to the bottom."

All people behave differently with different people. All people are different in different situations. We need to remember that obvious fact. My mother-in-law is a wonderful hostess but an uncomfortable guest. To put it another way, many people like to be in control of their surroundings and only then do they relax and let their full personality shine through. Children remain children in front of their parents even when the "children" are fifty years old, because they let themselves be cast in the "child" part in the "play" that is going on around them. The part we play, the role we accept or are given, affects the way we behave.

As I grow older I realize that the secret to much happiness and much achievement is to choose the roles that suit us, and only those roles. It is easier to do as one grows older, but it is made easier in part by a willingness to admit that some roles do not suit one. In early life there is either a natural ignorance or a natural arrogance that suggests that we can twist any role or any part to suit us. That is seldom true. The successful ones are those who, by luck or planning, find the roles that suit them early on and never try to play the parts they are not typecast for.

Similarly, in reverse, the secret to getting organized is to fit the personality to the part, or, sometimes, to adjust the part to the personality. Organizations that prescribe a set series of jobs for every entrant and then expect them to be successful in each are just plain silly. More sensible are the Japanese who practice the "horizontal fast track"; they put the more successful of their recruits into a rapid succession of different jobs on the same level in order to find out which areas and roles suit their talents best.

As individuals we should really put ourselves on some kind of horizontal fast track early in life. I am bemused by how many people just drift into careers and occupations, "because my father did it," or "because it turned up," and stay there for life, happy or unhappy, unaware that the plodding lawyer might have been a wow teacher, or the beleaguered bureaucrat a brilliant salesman. Changes that are forced on us in life can lead to new discoveries.

> Richard was the son of a minister, but he had put that behind him. He wanted the cut and thrust of business, the money, the excitement of foreign travel, the joy of conflict, not of caring. For thirty years he pursued his ambition with a succession of jobs in different organizations selling spirits or tobacco or property. Somehow he never made the top, or even the second layer. Continually frustrated, he would switch to a new company, with new hopes and high ambitions, only to find them squashed a few years later.
>
> He became an involuntary expert on job searching, on placement procedures, on interviews and recruitment procedures for middle managers.

> It seemed only natural that one day one of the headhunters he'd used to search out the latest of his jobs should offer him a job with the recruiting firm itself. The job, the recruiter explained, would be to act as a coach and a mentor to job-seekers like himself. With his experience and with his "helping, caring" attitude he would be able to offer them a lot. He accepted with enthusiasm: "It's just the job I want."
>
> His father must have chortled in his grave. So little do we really know ourselves or the roles that suit us.

Roles in life are one thing, roles in an organization are another. Few of us are as burdened as Pooh-Bah was in *The Mikado,* being simultaneously First Lord of the Treasury, Lord Chamberlain, Attorney General, Chancellor of the Exchequer, Privy Purse, and Private Secretary, and finding himself arguing with himself when his responsibilities came into conflict. However, anyone in charge of anyone else will find that their supposedly simple job is really a Chinese box of jobs, one within the other.

> "Well, I suppose that my main job is that of organizer. I have to make sure that all the *things* that are needed every day are actually here and in good condition. Then I have to see that each *person* in my care is where they ought to be, when they ought to be. But that is just for starters. I am then really a teacher and a coach because, if you think about it, my main mission is to see that each of them learns and grows as much as possible and performs to the limit of their ability. That would be fun but, of course, I also have to be judge as well as teacher, I have to reprimand as well as reward. I have to sort out arguments and conflicts and stop them coming to blows. Sometimes I have to impose my authority by sheer force of personality. Even that would be possible, but I then have my own work to get on with, telephones to answer, letters to deal with, contractors to be paid or hired, all as part of the day's work. Sometimes I feel that I ought to be five different people in five different places, all at once."
>
> "What do you do?"
>
> "I'm a mother."

Each little box in that Chinese box of a job requires something different from us. Nobody can be expert in all of them; the secret is to do more of what you do best, but that requires you to know each role and to be honest about yourself.

Another way of looking at a job is to see it as a web. You are the spider at the center but there are lines connecting you to everyone else with whom you have contact in that job. Some lines will be short and thick because the people are important to you and you have a lot to do with them. Some lines will be long and thin because the people are less crucial and the contact less frequent. Then there will be the odd line that is short but thin—infrequent contact with someone rather important (the boss's boss). It could look like this:

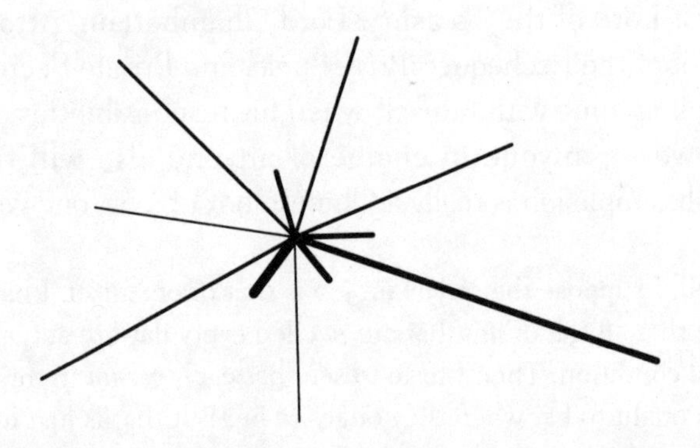

Amazingly, perhaps, it is not difficult to find twenty different people in this role web. The trouble is that each of the twenty will have a different view of you, a different set of expectations of you, and a slightly different relationship with you. There are, in effect, twenty different parts or roles for you to play, and you cannot be good at all of them. "Who am I?" you may be tempted to ask, when so many people see you differently. It is a good question indeed. One of the difficulties of working with any group of people is to remain true to yourself, or even to know which of the roles is really "you."

Like so many things in organizations, the possibility that people saw me differently from the way I saw myself, or that they might have different expectations of me from my own, was a blinding glimpse of the obvious. It is, however, crucially important. If we only talk to those we want to hear (the way of dictators down the ages), we shall hear nothing to surprise or dismay us, but we may miss out on some other crucial information. If we are to perform our job well, we need to know how others perceive our roles and our performance in them. Only then can we begin to either change our performance or to adjust their expectations of us.

> Roger was depressed. He had started the job with great enthusiasm. He was a newcomer to this department but he wanted to learn as well as manage and he wanted his section to feel that he was there to help as well as to plan and control.
>
> He was determined to be different from the rather cold and aloof supervisor whom he had succeeded—a man more feared than respected. Assiduously he practiced "management-by-walking-about," dropping in on people at their desks, asking for their ideas, trying to learn what they did in their jobs, trying to be informal and friendly. Somehow the theory did not work in practice. People did not smile back. Conversation died when he entered each room. He could not understand it. He was not a frightening person and he had made no unpopular decisions, nor intended to. He spoke to Marjorie, the personnel manager, one day. "It's not your job to walk about," she said. "When your predecessor did it, he went only to reprimand or check. They do not understand that you intend it in another way. You have to alter their picture of your role, because you have inherited your predecessor's role. You have to make it yours. I should start by just telling them why you're doing it. Some will believe it and gradually their view will infect the others."

Roger Harrison, a well-known management consultant, designed a most effective exercise to deal with the confusions of the role web. He called it Role Negotiation. It works like this:

Sit down with someone in your role web. Take three pieces of paper each. On one of them write down all the things you would like the other to do *more* of. On another, all the things you would like them to do *less* of. On the third, the things you want them to keep on doing just as they are. Then swap the bits of paper.

The third paper turns out to be a positive endorsement of much of what you are doing—so read that one first! The other two contain some practical advice, which you may or may not agree with. Roger Harrison suggests that you use the items on these two lists to do some trading with your partner, agreeing to do or stop doing some things in return for some equivalent changes on their side. It is, literally, a negotiation that ends with a new agreement.

The actual procedure of a Role Negotiation can be cumbersome but the ideas behind it are important. The role you have does not only affect you, it inevitably involves other people. The more you can bring their understanding of your role closer to your own, the better you will be able to perform it. Actors in the theater are helped by their director to understand their role. The rest of us seldom have that help. We have to do it on our own.

Most roles in life are given to us. We can then shape them to some extent, but the core duties of supervisor or manager, of nurse or inspector, even of father or mother, are already there. There is, however, the interpretation we give to that role, the character in the part, and this we can choose for ourselves. We can choose whether to be the comedian or the organizer, for example, or the commentator or the counselor, or just be the passive spectator, uninvolved and uninvolving. We can even shift from one character to the other in different groups, being the organizer at work but the counselor at home.

This choice of interpretation is more important than it seems. People take us at our word. If we take the comedian's part, they may laugh with us, but they will not think us capable of organizing unless we can slip into that role, too, on occasion. In ancient days actors wore masks. So do we all in real life. It is hard for the outsider to know the reality behind the mask, so choose your mask with care. The child who plays the rogue in his early days at school finds it hard to be taken seriously the next year. It is often easier to change the school than to change the mask. Nor is this any different for us adults.

SOME QUESTIONS FOR THINKING AND TALKING ABOUT

Getting organized is easier if *everyone* understands their role and the ways in which that role affects other people. It should never be assumed that others know what you know, or vice versa. The more explicit you can be, the better.

1. Do the exercises in this chapter. First draw your role web. Now pick a partner in your mind and do the Role Negotiation exercise mentally. What would you change in your behavior?
2. Do the same with your own work-group.
   a. Ask them to draw their role webs and compare results.
   b. Put them in pairs to do a trial Role Negotiation.
   c. Discuss the kinds of insights and problems that arose.
   d. List what changes need to be made to roles or to working habits.
3. What character (comedian, organizer, counselor, spectator) do you choose for yourself in the different parts of your life? Which would you change and how?

> "I watched Fiona Campbell-Walker on television describing her life as a top fashion model in the fifties and then her marriage to Baron Thyssen, one of the world's richest men.
>
> 'I tried very hard to be a good wife,' she said. 'I learnt Italian, French, and German as best I could. I entertained the people who were important to him and I tried always to look beautiful for him. I worked very hard at it and it was often lonely and difficult. When the divorce came, I asked him what had gone wrong.'
>
> 'You were so boring,' he said.
>
> Sometimes, with the best of intentions, we take our roles so seriously that we lose the person we really are."

8 Marathons or Horse Races

The start of the London Marathon, indeed of any marathon, is, I find, quite fascinating. Twenty thousand people in one race. They take ten minutes just to get through the starting gate. Crazy, when only one of them can win it. "You've missed the point," I was told when I said this to one of the runners. "It's not a horse race. We aren't trying to win the race, we are running against ourselves. Anyone who finishes is a winner."

Horse races and marathons, the difference is crucial. In a horse race the first three count and the rest are also-rans. In a marathon everyone who finishes "wins"; the aim for nearly everyone is only to better their previous time. The atmosphere at the end of a marathon, everyone exhausted but jubilant, is noticeably different from the end of a horse race, where one group is elated but most are dejected and disappointed.

We can regard different parts of life, and life itself, as a horse race or a marathon. Which we choose can matter enormously. Occasionally I get asked to speak at a school prize day. I always refuse, partly because I would not know what to say and partly because I feel uncomfortable watching so many people *not* getting prizes. It feels like an assembly of losers, not winners.

Examinations in British schools used to be organized on the horse race principle. It was called "norm referencing." The papers were all marked and then, at its simplest, the midpoint score was taken as the pass mark, the top ten percent as distinction and the next twenty percent as credit. By definition, under such a system, the bottom half failed, no matter how good they were. It was a mammoth horse race. The system was changed. Now the pass mark is set in advance; it is called "criterion referencing." Anybody who reaches that level passes, no matter how many of them there are. Indeed, in 1999, 45 percent of the entrants to the Latin "A" level examination got an A grade. It is now a marathon, a race that one day everyone will win. Very few people in Britain never pass their driving test; they may fail once, twice, or three times but in the end, with perseverance, they pass. No one thinks that the test is soft because everyone ultimately passes.

We can organize both life and organizations so that they are marathons or horse races. It is largely a matter of choice. Competition, after all, is around us. We cannot escape from competitors, but we can choose to see them as people who might beat us for the prize or as fellow runners.

Competition is useful. It sets standards. I was impressed, when visiting an East European country, to find that in a centrally planned economy, in a country of only ten million people, they had built three fertilizer plants, where economies of scale would have suggested just one big one. Indeed, they said, it might be more efficient, but *we* in the center would have to decide how to measure that efficiency. With three plants, the best one sets the standards for the others.

Competition stimulates energy. There is no doubt that people run harder in a race than they do in training. It is hard to rev yourself up when there is no one to compete with. Monopolies get lazy, as do the bits of organizations that are effectively monopolies—the accounting department, the audit office, the personnel department. All these are internal monopolies—at least the sales force has other sales forces to contend with.

Competition provides a purpose. Jogging can be tedious, and so can a lot of the repetitive grind of life and of work in an organization. No one can really enjoy putting nuts into a threading machine, one at a time, day in, day out. Provide some sort of scoring system, however, some competition and some prizes, and the work becomes a means to an end, not an end in itself.

But competition can destroy. Its main attraction, to some, lies in its ability to sort out the wheat from the chaff, to distinguish the poor performers and get rid of them. It is used as a sort of selective weedkiller, with the poorest withering. This sort of competition is divisive. It gets people worried, particularly if the punishment for losing is significant, like dismissal. Worried people start to play political games in order to protect themselves. More energy starts going into not losing rather than into winning. Competition has become conflict.

In their book, *In Search of Excellence,* Peters and Waterman reported some interesting forms of internal competition:

- 3M, Fluor, TI, and Bechtel operate "markets" internally for people wanting to be assigned to project teams so that the team leaders have to bid for the best people.
- Brands compete at Procter & Gamble.
- Digital, Hewlett-Packard, 3M, and Johnson & Johnson deliberately design company divisions and product lines so that their responsibilities overlap.
- Buyers and fashion coordinators compete for floor space at Bloomingdales.
- IBM encourages several groups to compete in solving the same problems.

Competition, in other words, is good news for everyone, but only if everyone can win. If success means a bigger cake and therefore bigger shares for everyone, that's OK—but if it means a bigger share for one and less for the others, then you get conflict and a waste of energy. It is quite possible that some of the competing groups listed by Peters and Waterman spent more time spying on each other or copying each other in case they missed a trick or two than they did on developing their own ideas.

Rosabeth Moss Kanter, a professor at Harvard, tells a chilling story in her book about large organizations, *When Giants Learn to Dance.* It happened at an AIDS laboratory in Atlanta. Highly paid professionals were accused of tampering with the experiments of their internal "competitors," of throwing away rivals' research materials, and of slowing down publication of key results. As she says, "when flasks with delicate virus cultures were rearranged and contaminated with human spit, and when other materials for examination ended up in the garbage, in-house competition had moved far beyond the point where it could be considered a spur to performance!"

She concludes, from her study of many large corporations, that cooperation *inside* the organization and competition *outside* is the best recipe for productivity. She is underlining the truth of the metaphor of this chapter: horse races are bad, marathons are good. External markets are marathons; everyone can do better, even if one or two do better than most. Internal competitions are horse races most of the time, because only one team or one person wins.

> Bluline, a fictitious name for a company selling household detergents, wanted to inspire its salespeople to greater achievements. It offered a holiday in Sardinia in a luxury villa with servants and all expenses paid to the family of the salesperson who produced the biggest increase in sales. Alec Mottaso won. He was delighted, but then embarrassed when the other salespeople accused him of fiddling the books by arranging for some of the preceding quarter's sales to be logged as this quarter's, thereby boosting his total in this quarter and reducing it in the earlier quarter, which would have been used as the base figure in the competition. He denied the charge but the slur stuck. In the end he turned down the holiday and later left the company. It took months to restore the morale of the sales force.
>
> The following year, Bluline offered the Sardinian holiday to anyone who could show a 20 percent increase, sustained for three quarters in succession. Ten out of the eighteen salespeople achieved it. The company had to rent three more villas to fulfill the bargain, but that was one bill the marketing director was delighted to pay.

Sales competitions are easy to turn into marathons. The competition for top jobs is less easy to handle in this way. Not everyone is in the same position as the head of one family business who was faced with choosing his successor from three very good executives, each one of whom could have done the job, but each of whom would, inevitably, be disappointed at losing out to one of the others, and might well leave the organization. "How did you resolve it?" I asked. "I appointed one and I bought another company for each of the others!" he replied.

The answer to the competition for top jobs is similar—create as many top jobs as possible. Organizations are becoming flatter, with more separate businesses, or separate activities, each reporting into a "center" rather than a "top"; each with its own leader or head; each competing with the others to raise the standards, to do better. In these organizations everyone can do better than their previous best, as in a marathon, and that is what counts. There can be medals for all, even if one also has a blue ribbon tied to it to signify that this was the best of the best.

When several thousand managers in America were asked about the circumstances in which they did their best, they did not talk about competition but about goals that were exciting and challenging, about autonomy and ownership, high visibility and accountability, and an exciting task. The thrill of the race was there, but it was the taking part that mattered, not the winning. Thus the "spirit of the Olympics" sometimes makes more sense in a work organization than in the Olympic stadium, where winning can sometimes be all that seems to matter. If you aren't up on that winner's podium you might as well not have bothered to come.

If marathon situations are impossible to arrange, avoid horse races wherever possible. In tough competitive situations, people like to be surrounded by people less competent than themselves because it gives them a better chance of winning. That is not good news for the organization. Nor do people always, or even often, take the risks or make the creative leaps that competition is supposed to encourage. The fear of failing is usually much stronger than the hope of winning, so people play safe.

> The man or woman who thought up the golf handicap was a psychological genius. Here is a game in which people actually strive to make winning more difficult for themselves! The handicap system is such that the lower your handicap, the more extra strokes you have to allow to your opponent. At the same time, all senior players are anxious to reduce their handicap to demonstrate that their game is improving. Golf, in other words, is a perpetual marathon, in which every player has the possibility of improving on a personal record, of winning even though each improve-

> ment is punctuated by the occasional defeat on handicap. Until he or she is almost perfect the average golfer never really loses. No wonder it is such a popular game.

In practice, most of the work we do is neither a marathon nor a horse race, it is just a trudge, not even as stimulating as a walk with the dog. However, it need not be. It does not require much ingenuity to build in the kind of milestones and targets that marathon runners need. They all carry watches, remember, and have a well-marked route to measure themselves against. Most of us, going on a familiar journey in a car, know how long it should take to reach certain points and take some satisfaction in keeping to our times. "Never taken more than one hour fifty minutes," boasted my neighbor, surely untrue, because I cannot do it in under two hours. Next time I will travel at 2 A.M. to see if I can match him!

We set up these daily marathons for ourselves in everyday life but neglect them in our organizations. We are stupid. It need not take much imagination or much effort and it *could* make life much more interesting, exciting, and productive for everyone.

SOME QUESTIONS FOR THINKING AND TALKING ABOUT

Getting organized is made much easier if you can arrange for work to be a series of marathons, or races against a personal record, rather than horse races.

1. Examine your own work. Pick out the three most important jobs you have to do over the next few weeks. Would you describe them as marathons, horse races, or just a trudge?
2. How could you turn them all into marathons?
   a. What markers are needed to allow you to measure improvement?
   b. Who can put them in place? Can you do it yourself?
3. Looking at the work of your subordinates, would you describe their key tasks as marathons, horse races, or neither? How could you change things?
4. Read some books on the subject. Tom Peters's books *In Search of Excellence* (Harper & Row, 1984) and *Thriving on Chaos* (Pan Books, 1989) are excellent value and easy reading for anyone interested in

exciting organizations. Rosabeth Moss Kanter's book *When Giants Learn to Dance* (Simon & Schuster, 1989) is a fascinating description of the best of the big U.S. corporations.

"'Done that,' he said, stepping onto the plane at Nairobi. 'That only leaves Nepal next summer.'

'What on earth are you talking about?' I said.

'I've crossed East Africa off my list, that's what I mean.'

'But it was great—the animals, the people, the scenery, that climb up Kilimanjaro—'

'Yes, of course, I loved it but now I don't need to do it again. It's my life list, things I need to have done. Don't you find that life's like that; things you want to do, but having done you don't need to do again, so you cross them off your list? What I don't know,' he said, 'is what happens when I get to the end of my list.'

'You're dead,' I said, 'so I hope you've got a good long list that isn't crossed off yet.'"

9 The Self-Fulfilling Prophecy

Researchers in the social sciences do odd things sometimes. Two of them, Robert Rosenthal and Lenore Jackson, stepped into a school—with permission, naturally. They gave a class of children an intelligence test and then fed back the scores to the class teacher. But they deliberately muddled up the scores! They gave high scores to some children in the middle layers and vice versa. The teacher did not know. They then monitored the classroom work for the next term. The middle-level kids with the high scores did very well indeed. Why? Because, said Rosenthal and Jackson, the teacher thought that they were intelligent, expected intelligent responses from them, and they lived up to the teacher's expectations.

Doubts have been cast both on the ethics of this piece of research and on its interpretation, but to me it is a nice story because it feels right. I know how hard I tried in my own youth not to let down a teacher who expected great things from me and how, occasionally, I would surprise myself in my achievements. The teacher's expectations of me raised my own.

It can, of course, work the other way. A friend was so annoyed by his demotion to a junior class in one subject that he worked like a demon to prove the teacher wrong. In this case the demotion contradicted his own expectation of himself—he could choose to change his self-image or he could change his performance. He decided to change his performance. I think that I would have shrugged my shoulders and given up the subject.

Prophecies, in other words, have a habit of coming true, simply because we work to make them true. It helps to remember this every day because it turns out to be a pleasant way to change people's behavior, as well as providing the clue to why well-intentioned efforts sometimes go wrong, because, inevitably, there are bad prophecies as well as good ones.

It all stems from our *image of ourselves.* We live with a small gap between the way we think we are and the way we would like to be, between our self-concept and our ideal. If the gap gets too big, if we are too far away from what we would like to be, we get depressed. If the gap is too small, if we are quite satisfied with the way we are, we have probably stopped trying and are sure to be intolerably smug and unbearable to others. This "image gap" will vary in different parts of our life. My self-concept of myself as a tennis player is very low, which used to make me very dispirited every time I played because I had dreams of screaming serves and immaculate volleys. Nowadays I have lowered my ideal and so am more comfortable with myself. On the other hand, I like to think that I am a good teacher, but could be even better. Both of these standards are set fairly high. As a result I can get exceedingly cross with myself when I fall below my own standards, nor is it any consolation to be told that it was still a great session by comparison with anyone else's. I am not comparing myself with anyone else, only with my potential self.

My ideal of myself
________________________(The way I would like to be)

THE IMAGE GAP

My self-concept ________________________
(The way I think I am)

All sorts of interesting things happen as a result of this simple diagram. Take what is called *attribution theory,* for instance. It says, quite simply, that we like to take credit for the good things we achieve and to blame someone or something else for the failures. Obvious, but we turn out to be quite ingenious in our excuses.

> Virginia was supposed to be a teenage star in mathematics. Everyone expected her to do wonderfully well in her examinations that summer. Virginia, however, was not so confident. Too much, she felt, might be expected of her. She stopped work, she stayed out late at parties, she slept late in the mornings, she missed class. Her parents were frantic, her teachers worried. They harangued her, they pleaded, they encouraged, they bullied. All to no avail. Virginia seemed dejected, uninterested, almost willing herself to fail. She didn't fail, but she didn't do nearly as well as she might have.
>
> "What went wrong, Virginia—surely you're smarter than that?"
>
> "Of course I am, I just couldn't be bothered. Silly old maths. Who cares?"
>
> Virginia was carefully protecting her rather fragile ideal of herself as a clever girl. By blaming boredom and social distractions she was able to attribute her lack of success to something else. She could then go on claiming to herself that she was clever. Being wise, with hindsight, her parents and teachers should have lowered their expectations, allowing her to lower her own ideal of herself. She would not then have needed to provide herself with excuses in advance and might have worked quite normally. Expectations, in other words, can be set *too* high.

You can, however, use the attribution theory in a positive way, relying on the fact that we are only too happy to take the credit for any good news. Take the case of Roger, an insurance salesman. When Roger's manager gave him the credit for a major sales boost in his area, Roger's self-concept was lifted a good half-inch, pushing up his ideal and his ambitions. Believing himself to be very capable, he set high standards and achieved them. And, as they were new standards that he had set himself, he was not likely to start devising excuses in advance in case he failed. Moral: people must set their own ideals if they are going to take them seriously. On the other hand, however, take the "Case of the Appraisal Interview":

> It is Roger again, two years later—still successful, still boosting sales. His manager has arranged the annual appraisal interview with him. He is pleased with him but would like him to do even better and, besides, there are one or two complaints about his high-handed treatment of the administrative staff.
>
> "It has been a good year, Roger," the manager began, "all targets met, and ahead of time. Well done." Roger smiled. "Of course," he went on, "you had the new product advertising to help you, and I wanted to say a word about that."
>
> "Really?" Roger scowled.
>
> "Yes, they have been complaining in the office that they found it difficult to get information out of you about the new sales locations and that, on occasion, you came across as rather high-handed. I thought that maybe I could set up a little meeting with them, with myself in the chair, to sort things out."
>
> "I don't know what you're talking about," Roger said. "They've never said anything to me. Can you give me chapter and verse?"
>
> "Well, no, not precisely, it's just a general attitude they talk about."
>
> "If it's attitudes that we are discussing," retorted Roger, "I can tell you a bit about theirs. I'm also rather surprised that you should take their side."
>
> "Come on," said the manager. "I was only trying to help, to help you do an even better job next year."
>
> "Oh, sure! I thought it was all the product advertising that did it. Well, next year, I can tell you, I'm going to keep those targets realistic, and I'm going to have it out with the office." Roger left, still muttering.

Good intentions so often fall foul of the image net. Roger is concerned to keep his self-concept where it is—high. His manager wants to do likewise, but inadvertently attributes some of Roger's success to others. He then gives Roger a suggestion about his behavior that, although intended to help, begins to push his self-concept down a bit. The manager hopes that Roger will, as a mature person, say, "Gosh, thank you, I need to mend my ways so that my self-concept remains where it is." Instead Roger wants to deny the message he is receiving. He does this first by denying the evidence, then by denigrating the other party, and finally by denigrating his manager. That way he can say to himself that the message is false or from unreliable sources, and therefore he need take no notice of it. Attribution theory has worked. His self-concept is undamaged. Unfortunately, in the process, he has lowered his opinion of his manager and his colleagues, and has decided to keep his targets safely down for the next year.

The interview was a disaster, but quite unintentionally. Unfortunately, all too many interviews of this type, which start with such good intentions, end with the recipient leaving in sulks, in no mood to accept the advice he has been offered, and with less respect for his manager or the organization.

Our self-concept is a fragile thing. We do all we can to protect it. Consider now the theory of "dissonance reduction," grand words for a process of unconscious rationalization we all go through to keep our prophecies self-fulfilling and our self-concept intact.

It works like this: having made a decision, we automatically look for evidence to support our decision and block out any other data. Whenever I screw up my courage (and my money) and buy a new car, it's then that I start to read all the advertisements, but only those for my car, not the other ones. It is a subconscious way of reassuring myself that I did the right thing. That way I reduce the *dissonance,* or disagreement, between what I have done and what I perhaps should have done, like buy another make.

Roger was doing the same in his interview. He did not want to hear what his boss was telling him so he chose to discount the evidence and to downgrade his respect for his boss. That way he need not pay attention to the "dissonant" information.

The theory, put like that, sounds obvious, but it produces some surprising results. Students and new army recruits often have to endure humiliating initiation ceremonies when they join a fraternity or a regiment. Called *hazing,* it is the sort of public bullying which no one in their right mind would want to undergo. After it is over, however, the great majority say that it was a good thing. Why? Because if it was wholly bad, they should have refused to do it. Since they did not refuse, the only way to maintain their self-respect and their self-concept is to find good reasons for thinking it a sensible thing to do, and therefore, in turn, to do it to their successors.

Some cynics say that this accounts for the fact that 90 percent of participants of *any* training program rate it as worth attending. "Well, they would, wouldn't they?" says dissonance theory, otherwise they should have got up and left. Few of us can bring ourselves to say, "I did this. It was a complete waste of time for me. You should not have to do it." Human beings are complicated. We do not always do or say the obvious, sensible things. Dissonance theory—the need to keep our self-concept intact—often tells us why.

> I had just got engaged. Ecstatic about my bride-to-be, I had to show her off to my old school and college friends. They were not all as enthusiastic as I was about her. Looking back, some of this was, no doubt, the touch of jealousy we all feel when an old friend loses their heart to someone outside the gang. At the time I resented it, particularly the comments which started, "As an old friend, I can tell you this. . . ." As I saw it, I had to choose between my friends and my bride. My bride won! I ceased to see some of my old friends. Now I understand that I could not handle the dissonance—if I think X is OK and my friends do not, there is dissonance. I could reduce it by changing my mind or by denigrating them as friends, *or* I could decide to live with the dissonance, which is what I would do today. If they don't like the way I live that is their problem; they can still be my friends, there are just some things we will agree not to agree about. My self-concept is unaffected—but it is more resilient now than it was then!

We can turn all these theories to good effect in our relations with other people, particularly people over whom we have some influence or who hold us in any sort of respect: our subordinates, our pupils, our family, our colleagues. People who feel good, do good. This is the first and most important interpretation of the self-fulfilling prophecy. Boost our self-concept and we will do our best to live up to it: boost our self-concept by loading it with praise (more on this in Chapter Ten); boost it by raising our "ideal" of what we might be, so that we begin to pull our self-concept up after it; convince us that we are capable of greater things. We shall, if we believe you, try to prove you right.

Do not do the negative things. Do not bash our self-concept by ill-founded criticism. Remember that feedback, to be accepted, must be (a) specific, related to some recent event, (b) backed by very obvious evidence, and (c) given by someone whom we respect and regard. I will take criticism from my golf instructor about my swing because I respect his skill, he can demonstrate where I have gone wrong immediately after the event, and I know he wants me to improve. I am less sure about some bosses I have had!

Remember, however, that everyone else wants to respect their own self-concept as well and will make sure that prophecies they make to themselves turn out right. They will, therefore, avoid any evidence they don't like, or any people who may prove them wrong. You should not, therefore, expect your version of the truth to be what other people want to hear if it is going to damage their self-concept.

On the other hand, if it improves their self-concept, the truth can produce wonderful results.

> Angie, the world said, was a cripple, or in today's more acceptable language, physically handicapped. Her legs did not function after a car crash. She was twenty-five, beautiful, with her life in ruins. She took to her bed and became an invalid. Lying there she heard a broadcast one morning. "We are all handicapped in some way," the speaker was saying. "It depends on you whether you focus on your handicap—your ugly face, your baldness, your lack of qualifications, your limp, your sex, or your age—or whether you focus on your talents and abilities. After all, Beethoven was deaf, and Julius Caesar was squat, bald, and ugly at thirty-five." Angie wrote to the broadcaster a few weeks later; "I'm a full-time student of computing now," she said, "with a super boyfriend and we have just arranged to go on a camping holiday in France. It sounds ordinary enough, maybe, but for me it's life after death—all because your talk that morning made me get out of bed—thank you."
>
> Nothing had changed except her self-concept, but that had changed everything.

SOME QUESTIONS FOR THINKING AND TALKING ABOUT

Getting organized requires that you do your best to create self-fulfilling prophecies for yourself and for everyone around you, by boosting their self-concept and protecting them from too much damage.

1. How do you react to criticism? Be honest with yourself. Think of an occasion when the criticism was really justified but you rejected it because it was too damaging to your self-concept. Do this exercise in privacy. Talk about it only if you want to.
   a. How did you explain the criticism away?
   b. How could you have been helped to take the criticism on board without damage to your ideals or to your image of yourself?
2. What are your own ideals, in work, in life? It helps to be as specific as you can, looking perhaps ten years ahead.
   a. What do you need more of to help you reach those ideals?
   b. Which of those skills, talents, and abilities are currently underused or underappreciated?
   c. What are you going to do about it?
3. Take the people who are closest to you, for whom you have responsibility. It might be your partner in life and your child. It might be your principal subordinates or colleagues. If the relationship between you and them is strong enough, ask them to go through the same process, first for themselves, then for you. Compare your results. Why are they different (if, indeed, they are)? What can you jointly do about them?

“John was cutting the hedges along the lane with his big mechanical cutter. It was his first year on the job. Previously Stephen had been under contract to do all the hedges and ditches in the area, but he had decided to change career and become a builder. We were sad because we had delighted in the clear ditches and borders, and in the way he trimmed the hedges but left them full and tall.

John was doing a good job. I stopped to congratulate him.

‘Looks perfect,’ I said. ‘It’s a nice job you’re doing on it.’

‘I’m following a perfectionist,’ he said. ‘I’ve got to live up to Stephen.’

No formal objectives here, I thought, just an example. Examples are, maybe, the very best way of setting standards—if they are good enough, that is.”

10 The Stroking Formula

Scott was pleased with himself. He had formed this dance band at his college. They would play at dances, arrange gigs, maybe even get a record contract one day.

"Much more fun than working in a shop," he said, "and probably more profitable. I'm running a very tight ship," he told me. "No shirkers or slackers allowed. I really tear a strip off them if they turn up late."

"And does that work?" I asked.

"Not yet, the lazy devils; they just scowl and mutter, but they'll find out that I'm tougher than they think. It's the only way to do it. Julian, for instance, who is meant to do the bookings, is incredibly lazy. I've just had to shout at him constantly to get him off his backside. It's hard work running things, I find."

"Yes," I said, "shouting is exhausting, and expensive, and inefficient."

"What do you mean?" Scott asked. "What else can I do?"

I explained.

It is natural to want to shout at someone when they do something wrong. Or, if you don't like raising your voice, a bit of pained exasperation, patient reproof, or even the teacher's favorite tool, sarcasm, can be just as cutting.

"How many times have I told you—?" "And just what do you think you are doing—?" "If I find you once more—?" "How can you be so stupid as to—?" "Give me one good reason why—?" The phrases trip off the tongue very rapidly, the tone of voice says it all. "You did wrong. You deserve to be punished."

And it works—for a time. No one likes to be shouted at, or even reprimanded. We will do our best to avoid it in future. One way, the logical way, is to change our behavior, to do things the right way, the way the person wants them done. Unfortunately, human beings are not always logical, they are psychological, they think with their feelings as much as their brains. The other way to avoid being shouted at is to avoid being caught.

If you run a shouting regime, you have to be a police officer as well. You have to check, endlessly, constantly, that your wishes are being obeyed. Even if people do not cheat but genuinely try to do it right, they may well not try so hard when you are gone; it is *your* wishes they are carrying out, *your* rules, *your* commands, and when you are no longer there, the wishes, rules, and commands can easily disappear with you. It is because shouting implies checking that it in the end becomes inefficient, and therefore expensive. There *are* other ways.

> Teachers often complained about the increasing difficulty of keeping order in the classroom. They blamed it on the growing rowdiness of society, on fashionable disrespect for authority, on parents who no longer disciplined their children, on anything except themselves.
>
> A research study, however, sent observers into the classrooms. The observers counted the number of times teachers commended or praised a student and the number of times they reprimanded or punished one. In total the teachers praised and reprimanded about equally, but all the praise was for academic work and all the reprimands were for behavior.
>
> The researchers then took a group of teachers away and coached them in a new way of reacting to behavior. Ignore bad behavior, they said, but pick out any and every instance of correct behavior for commenda-

> tion. It was hard to do and not every teacher managed it or could keep it up, but those who did found that disruptive behavior decreased dramatically after about three weeks back in their classrooms. It had become fashionable to be well behaved, it seemed.

The truth is that we all are insecure at heart, we all respond positively to being stroked, psychologically stroked, that is. And stroking lasts longer than striking. Anything that produces good vibes is something that we will cultivate because we will want to claim that good behavior is part of ourselves. I make whole wheat bread. People compliment me on it and wolf it down. I make more and boast about it. I call myself a home baker. I am proud of it and cultivate it because it seems to be a part of me that goes down well. And I go on baking bread, although no one asks me to, although it would be easier to buy it in the shops and probably cheaper, although it is time-consuming and difficult to fit into my day. If it were my *duty* to make the bread, if decent loaves were taken for granted and I was scolded when the bread was bad, or late, or missing, why then baking would be a chore. I wouldn't do it if I could avoid it and, once the family was away, I would buy all my loaves from the shop.

It is obvious really. Carrier pigeons learn quickly to go to the home where they are stroked and fed. If we are sensible we train dogs by rewarding good behavior, not by punishing bad. If your dog wanders off when it shouldn't, when you call it and it comes, do you punish it (for wandering off) or pat it (for coming when called)? If you punish it, you may well end up with a more devious dog that wanders off without your discovering, or a dog that does not come when called because experience shows that the likely result is a whipping. Humans are not that different. "I try to catch people doing something right," said Kenneth Blanchard in *One-Minute Manager.* It is a good motto for all would-be strokers.

What, then, does one do when people break the rules? "Make them pay the penalty" has to be the answer. But it would be better still if they did not break the rules or even want to. All organizations have rules, all households need rules, even if they are as basic as "Lock the door when you go out" or "Turn out the lights." At work there are forms to be filled in, deadlines to be kept, quality standards to be maintained, plans to be made and schedules to be met. If people understand the reasons for these rules, if they helped to make them, if they benefit when they go well or suffer when they go wrong, then the rules become self-maintaining. One's own rules are good sense, other people's rules are a nuisance.

> Most drivers, today, automatically fasten their seat belts. Yet most drivers break the speed limit every day. Is it because the police are better at enforcing the seat-belt law than the speed limit? No. We know that if we break the seat-belt rule it is ourselves who suffer in an accident, whereas a small excess of speed helps us and hinders no one, we hope. The seat-belt laws are self-enforcing, speed limits need policing. Drinking and driving laws will work much better if people are convinced of their good sense and do not see them as an arbitrary infringement on their freedom.

It is the same in the office, or even in the home. Rules are self-enforcing when it is the rule breaker who is the first to suffer.

> My teenage children are, like most at their age, telephone addicts. We lectured them on the cost of calls. They forgot the lectures. We rationed the length of calls—to their great annoyance. They overran the ration if we were not around. We installed a timer. They found a way to fix it. We locked the telephone. They unlocked it when we were not looking. We appealed to their good sense. They argued that our priorities were misplaced; conversation, relatively, they said, was a cheap habit, better than alcohol or drugs. In the end I gave them a telephone of their own. I paid for the second phone line and gave them $25 a quarter to cover essential calls and put the telephone in their name so that they got all the bills. They were very grateful for this piece of personal freedom. I saved a lot of money, but I also noticed that their bills seldom exceeded the $25 I donated. They made a new rule for themselves—everyone should phone them, not the other way round; that way someone else's parents paid for their conversational relaxation. It was their rule, not my rule, so they kept it because it was they who suffered if they broke it.

Most organizations are timetable organizations. That is, they draw up a nice tidy set of rules and regulations, procedures and systems, and then try to make sure that everyone sticks to them. Unfortunately, the rules are almost always "other people's rules," they are not owned or designed or valued by the players in the game. Therefore the rules are not self-regulating, they need policing. In timetable organizations good work is unnoticed work; it is doing nothing wrong, making no mistakes, keeping to the book. It is bad work that gets noticed—noticed and penalized. In these organizations you go home happy at the end of the week if your work has caused no comment, if nothing went wrong. But it is a sterile sort of happiness, an emptiness of pain rather than a rush of joy. Timetable organizations are often soulless places, places where even a strike can be a pleasant break from the routine.

It does not have to be that way. I once asked an official at the railway station in Bonn, West Germany, why they had no station clock. "We have a timetable, over there," he pointed, "you can tell the time by our trains." He meant that when the 9:41 train from Cologne drew in you could be sure that it was 9:41, clock or no clock. I do not know, but I suspect that in that organization sticking to the timetable was a matter of honor and pride, and often of congratulation. So it is that good businesses today have started to put quality at the top of their priorities, insisting that it is not good enough to get it right *most* of the time. There has to be a standard of zero defects—but it has to be a matter of pride, not a rule to be policed, or it will never be achieved.

Zero defects are taken for granted in some organizations. We should learn from them. No mother would willingly go to have her baby in a maternity hospital that boasted of a 95 percent success rate. She wants 100 percent and the hospital expects it too, as a matter of honor and of pride. The doctors and nurses in the maternity wards are not about to conceal dead babies or to shortchange the mothers in their care, or, if they do, it becomes a national scandal. The key rules in such organizations are self-enforcing, relying not on policing but on good education, effective training, and the reward of good relationships with others. Every healthy newborn baby, every beaming parent, is an effective pat on the back for doctors, midwives, and nurses. The baby is the stroke.

It is not as easy in other organizations, but it is not impossible. Where good work carries its own obvious reward, rules are self-regulations, organizational police officers are unnecessary, pats on the back by superiors are superfluous (although welcome), standards are things to be exceeded, not just hoped for. If, therefore, one could redesign an automobile plant so that a team of people built each car and then delivered it to the customer, the maternity ward phenomenon would be replicated. It is not impossible. Volvo has done it. It costs more in the short run, but in the long run you get better people, working better, with less supervision needed.

There is one caveat to all the advice in this chapter—the praise, the stroking, and the rewards for achievement must all be truly felt and be based on truly good results. None of us like to be manipulated and to be praised for what we know, deep down, is low-grade work. This will only arouse the cynic in us. "What does he want from me?" has to be one's secret question, even while you accept the compliment. It is also ineffective manipulation, for all the research shows that praising people does not make them like you any more. Praise only makes them feel better if they think that they deserve it.

SOME QUESTIONS FOR THINKING AND TALKING ABOUT

Getting organized efficiently requires that you work out your own stroking formula for those you are responsible for.

1. Have you made any new rules recently—at work or in the home?
   a. Are they self-enforcing or does someone have to check that they are being obeyed?
   b. How could they be made more self-enforcing? Think creatively!
2. Discipline your reactions. Count the compliments and praise you distribute over a week.
   a. Did you do enough of the complimenting, was it specific, and was it genuine?
   b. If there was not much of it, why was that?

   This little bit of recording is a useful discipline for parents as well as for managers, for teachers as well as heads of schools, for civil servants, and police officers, too.
3. Can you find a way of redesigning the work of a group so that they experience all the satisfaction and frustration of completing a whole job and have control as far as possible of their own costs and income? Start with your own job.

   This exercise, too, is not irrelevant to the work of the home or the classroom.

"'I've got a job,' Jenny said, 'and I've found a day-care center for Johnnie.'

'What do you want to do that for?' said Dick, her husband. 'Johnnie needs you, and besides, day-care centers, as you call them, cost money.'

'Don't worry about the money—my salary will cover that, *and* my travel expenses, *and* my lunches. I've worked it all out. There won't be any left over, after tax, but there will be enough to cover the costs.'

'I don't understand,' Dick was frowning, 'if you don't make any extra money, what's the point of all the effort? Aren't you happy at home?'

'Yes, I'm happy enough—but I need something else. I need to prove that I'm competent still, that I can do more than raise kids and keep house. I need to prove myself to myself, and I also need some recognition from my peers. Johnnie's smiles are great, but I could do with some adult appreciation.'

'I love you, don't I?'

'Of course you do, but that's not the only appreciation I need.'

Everyone needs strokes, of all sorts, every day."

11 Parents, Adults, and Children

"Where did I put my car keys?" he asked.

"Just think," she said, "when you came in, did you go to the kitchen or did you forget them, as you often do, and leave them in the car? You really ought to be more tidy-minded, then you wouldn't have to waste time in looking."

"Where did I put my car keys?" he asked, on another day.

"Don't look at me," she said, "I haven't touched them. I haven't even seen them, honestly."

"Where did I put my car keys?" he asked, on yet another day.

"On the table—over there," she said.

"Thank you," he said.

The same question, asked on three different days, with three very different responses; all examples of the little games we play with each other, usually unconsciously, all the time. On the first occasion, she responded as the scolding, tutoring parent, probably because he asked in a petulant voice, like a complaining child. On the second day, it is she who responds as a petulant child, perhaps because he asked the question like an angry parent. On the third day, she gives a straightforward adult reply to an adult question.

The parent, the child, and the adult are all there, somewhere, in each of us. At least that is the theory of Eric Berne, who wrote the best-selling book *Games People Play,* back in 1964, in which he delivered a whole approach to relationships called transactional analysis. To me, the flash of insight was not only that there are different bits of us, the parent, the adult, and the child, but that each of the bits can pop out in all sorts of different situations, sometimes usefully, sometimes disastrously. A little understanding of what was going on has, I found, helped enormously, although I still cannot always produce the right bit of me to order!

Berne makes the point, and it is an important point, that we need each of these three parts to be whole. The child in us, for instance, can be the creative, curious, impulsive being as well as the one who reacts by whining, rebelling, or acting stubborn. The parent in us is the part that wants things to be under control, that wants order and stability as well as growth and development. The parent in us says, "Because that's the way it's done," even while the child in us asks, "Why is it that way?" The adult bit of us is our mature, rational, problem-solving side. It is necessary to keep the adult, parent, and child in some sort of balance. Too much parent and we lose the spontaneity and fun of the child, while too much of the reactive child stops us from developing our full potential. The mature person is a PAC man or PAC woman, a decent bit of parent, adult, and child.

The games start when one PAC person meets another PAC person in any kind of interaction or transaction (hence transactional analysis). Line the PACs up against each other. There are nine possible combinations. No wonder relationships get complicated.

It would be nice to think that we all, as grown-up people, use the adult bit of us in every transaction and get an adult response in reply. But, of course, it does not work out like that. An adult approach may trigger a

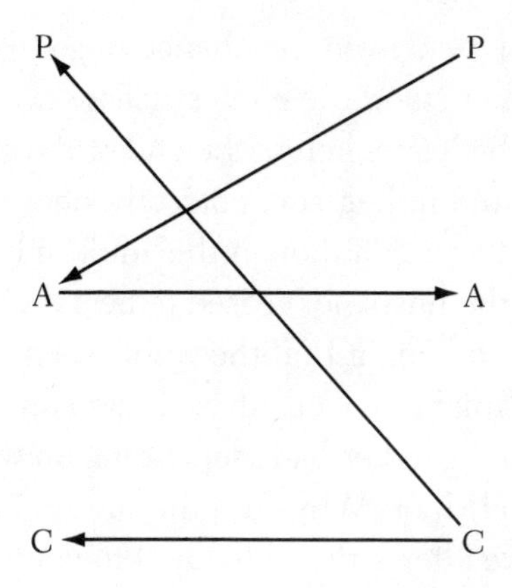

child response, and vice versa, as one part of us transacts with a different part of someone else.

Here is an example of one of Berne's simpler games—the sales game.

Car salesman: This one is better, but you can't afford it.
Customer: That's the one I'll take.

It is a clever ploy. On the surface the salesman is talking as an adult to an adult and telling the objective truth. No sales pitch at all. Underneath the surface, however, he is speaking as an adult to a child—at least, that is the way it feels to the customer, who reacts as a child, asking for what seems to be out of reach. Because, however, the words come out of his grown-up face, the salesman is entitled to assume that the customer is speaking as an adult. He makes the sale. The customer can't complain. The salesman told him the truth! The car really was beyond his means but the child in him was not interested in the truth.

Games are serious things, not all fun by any means, but they can explain many of the dilemmas we get ourselves into. "If it weren't for him," is one such game. In this a wife, or it could be a husband or a subordinate, complains that if it weren't for her demanding husband, she could go back to college—or get a job, play more bridge, or whatever her secret dreams have been. Later, given the chance to go to college, she then discovers that she cannot stand the endless class sessions and is terrified of the examinations. She leaves before the end of the course. What has happened is that the child in her, very correctly, chose the kind of husband who would control her life, although the adult in her chafes at this from time to time. If he, the husband, ceased to be a tough parent and became a consenting adult, she might find the whole scene too threatening. This is a game that they might be well advised to go on playing.

Some games are good or bad, depending on which bit of us is playing them. Take WAHM, or "Why does this always happen to me?" Played as a child, this game allows the individual to complain that he or she is always a victim. Even if they are not, they will push events so far that something is bound to go wrong; then, once again, they can cry WAHM and get the sympathy and reassurance they crave from indulgent parents all around. Played as an adult, however, the trial of misfortunes is a trigger for a piece of useful reflection and self-criticism, which can result in a resolve to change one's behavior so that it does *not* "always happen to me."

Games, in other words, can be healthy and good for us. Executives, for instance, used to be encouraged to let the creative child out of themselves more often, for their own benefit and for the good of the organization. Some organizations, therefore, go out of their way to create temporary "playpens"—in some comfortable resort hotel, as often as not—where uniforms and status signs are swept away, where brainstorming groups are allowed to be as ingenious as they like, where party games are encouraged and slanderous lyrics laughed at in the late-night revels. It would not do to behave like this in the office where adults and parents parade, so the whole event is safely off-site and the players return, suitably suited and sober-faced, on Monday morning, having discovered another side to themselves, and to each other, and having made some creative contributions to corporate thinking. The child in us nearly always needs corporate encouragement.

Robert Fulghum summed up the wisdom of the child in his little book, *All I Really Need to Know I Learned in Kindergarten.*

> Most of what I really need to know about how to live, and what to do, and how to be, I learned in kindergarten. These are the things I learned:

> share everything; play fair; don't hit people; put things back where you found them; clean up your own mess; don't take things that aren't yours; say you're sorry when you hurt somebody; wash your hands before you eat; . . . live a balanced life, learn some and think some and draw some and paint and sing and dance and play and work every day some; take a nap every afternoon; when you go out into the world, watch for traffic; hold hands and stick together; be aware of wonder.

Whereas the child in us needs encouraging, the parent in us often needs restraining. It is hard, as any father or mother knows, to stop fathering and mothering one's young, even when they are no longer that young. Inevitably, the grown-up children will react as children, not as adults, and as resentful children at that. I can recall only too vividly how quickly I, a grown man with wife and children, became my mother's little boy whenever I visited her. I remember her waiting up for me at night when I was twenty-eight years old and out for the evening. I remember being none too pleased at this sign of maternal care and being unnecessarily rude to her.

We are not any better in organizations, almost relishing any chance to play the wise owl, the godparent, the counselor, the teacher, or the judge; ready with the helpful piece of advice, the timely warning, the kindly admonition. It is all necessary, no doubt, and well intended, but it can so often be heard as the parent talking to a child, who then behaves as a child might, resentful, sulky, or even rebellious. Sometimes it is just the tone of voice that needs to change; more often it is an attitude of mind.

> I once visited a psychotherapist for consultations. Each consultation started on the hour and ended after fifty minutes, at ten minutes to the hour. Once I was twenty minutes late, held up by a traffic jam. At ten to the hour the little clock pinged. The psychotherapist stood up to signal that the consultation had ended.
>
> "But I haven't had my fifty minutes," I exclaimed. "Is anybody coming after me?"
>
> "No," he said, "but your time is finished."
>
> "But I started late," I said. "It was the traffic. It delayed me unavoidably."
>
> "That's your problem," he said, "not mine."

I seethed. On reflection, however, it was the most important lesson I learned from him. I habitually took responsibility for other people's problems. I would certainly have changed my schedule to accommodate his if our roles had been reversed. I have even heard myself apologizing to foreigners for the English weather, as if it was my fault! I loved, in fact, finding any chance to become the responsible parent, if someone else would be the child. Now, I know, stealing people's problems is nearly always wrong.

We cannot, however, help being parents, in real life or in organizations, as we begin to assume responsibility. The trick is to keep the parent role in the background so that the children in our care can learn to behave as adults. Some parentlike attitudes, however, we would do well to cultivate. We must, for instance, learn to live vicariously, as parents have to do, and teachers too, getting our satisfaction privately from others' successes but not stealing the credit, even though a lot of it may be due to us. We must take private satisfaction from hearing them say things and watching them do things we gave them or taught them, without reminding them where they learned them. We must, as parents, want them to be themselves and live their own lives, not be some copy of ourselves. We must, too, as parents, recognize that there will be a time when they are better than we are, and we must not try to deny that time when it has come.

Hal was my earliest mentor. It was he who first spotted me in the depths of the organization, twenty years ago, gave me my first real job and helped me learn my trade. He was a real friend and my organizational godfather.

Then I left to be a teacher. Hal was furious.

"You had a great future, you have thrown it away."

I meet him still, occasionally. He still shakes his head sadly over me. "I heard you on the radio, last week," he would say. "Such a pity."

"What do you mean?"

"You could have been a general manager by now, in the Philippines, for instance."

"But I never wanted to be a general manager in the Philippines."

"You would have, if you had stayed."

He is not my mentor any more, and nostalgia, overdone, gets tedious.

One common game in organizations is "doctors and patients." It was Ivan Illich in his book *Disabling Professions* who pointed out that doctors, and all professionals, are more interested in patients they can help and diseases they can cure than in the ones they can't. There is, therefore, a tendency for them to make the diagnosis fit their skills or even, as Illich suggests, to have a vested interest in inventing illnesses they can cure. All experts, be they doctors, teachers, or business consultants, are to some extent sometimes in search of problems they can solve, however much they may protest the opposite. There are also people only too willing to be that problem or that patient; it is a most acceptable adult/child situation.

Trainers, therefore, do not find it hard to find students, nor internal consultants willing customers. The trouble is that they may not be the right students nor the right customers. Too many training courses are attended by people who do not need to be there, too many consultants are employed by people who know what they are going to be told before they start. It is, however, a comforting relationship, with interest and good feelings for all concerned, and because no one involved is likely to complain, the collusion continues. It is not evil, but it is often unnecessary. "Never be seduced by weakness," I was wisely advised when I first started to work as an adviser to organizations. "The people who want you most are probably the people who are most ineffective. You will be welcomed by them, may even help them, but it will do the organization little good." Comfort can be deluding.

In each of us there is a parent, an adult, and a child. No one is, or should be, an adult all the time. There are good parents and bad, good childlike behavior and disruptive behavior. It is important to remember all these things. Remember, too, that parentlike behavior can bring out the child in people, and vice versa.

There are no "get rich quick" recipes in all of this. Awareness is all, awareness of the parts each is playing in each little game. Awareness makes one more tolerant, awareness helps one avoid some bad scenes, awareness can help one bring the best out in other people. I found, myself, that I started to look with new eyes at people talking to each other. It was fascinating.

SOME QUESTIONS FOR THINKING AND TALKING ABOUT

Getting organized is helped by an understanding of what is going on when people meet.

1. Reflect on three important meetings or conversations in which you were involved during the last two or three weeks.
   a. What parts (parent, adult, or child) were played by each participant?
   b. Could the parts have been changed (from parent to adult, or from, say, tough parent to indulgent parent) and would that have made any difference?
2. Imagine the next important event in your life or work.
   a. How do you intend to handle it?
   b. Having read this chapter, could you do it any differently?
   c. Will you? How?
3. If you want to see more about this topic, read Eric Berne's *Games People Play,* published by Penguin Books.

"Boris was not my wife's favorite man, but I had known Boris from long ago, from my days in the jungles of the Far East, long before I met my wife. We had shared experiences she knew not of, had drunk strange drinks in strange places, and so, although it was years since we had gone down separate paths in life, I still liked to see him every few months. Old friends are good friends, I said.

'You are very strange when you are with him,' she said. 'You are not yourself. I don't know what it is, but you pretend to be someone else, and you let him trample all over you, patronize you almost. It's as if you were his son, the way you look for his approval.'

'Maybe,' I said, 'maybe, way back, I did treat him as a sort of mentor. He was wise in the ways of the world then. Maybe I've never grown out of that habit.'

'Well, I don't like it. It doesn't suit you. You should not play that game.'"

12 Power Politics

"Oh for a world without politicking," I used to sigh when I worked in business. "Oh for a world where people told it the way it is, where everyone got on with the job, where reason and sensible discussion led to decisions, where there were no cabals, no locked doors, no secrets inside the organization." I left to work in a university. It was worse, much worse. I left to work with a church. It was worse, much worse. It took me a long time to realize that power and politics are part of life in organizations everywhere. We have to learn to live with them—and the more we understand them, the better we will be able to cope.

Language is important here. Power is not a good word. It has overtones of feudalism. No one wants to admit to having power, but we can all see that it's around. It is also grammatically a strange word. There is no verb to go with it. You cannot "power" people to do something, and so, when we want to talk about using power we have to use quite different words such as *controlling* or *influencing* or *directing*. Odd. And confusing.

We use words like *authority* when we want to suggest that our power is legitimate, and words like *influence* when we want to imply that you are free to reject our suggestions. In practice, however, whatever words we use to cover it up, there are only three useful kinds of power to draw upon if we want to make something happen. If you cannot count on any of the three, then you will be effectively powerless to affect events—with one great exception: almost everyone in an organization, from highest to lowest, has some *negative power,* but more about that later.

- *Resource Power:*
  The control over guns or money or property gives you the ability to influence events, most obviously when you are a terrorist with a gun or when you own something vital. Brute force, muscles, the use of physical intimidation are all more common than we might think in some organizations, and all too frequent in some homes. These are all forms of resource power. Common, too, is psychological intimidation, the kind of bullying that powerful personalities find all too easy. We don't need to be big to frighten people.
- *Position Power:*
  The title or role you have entitles you to issue instructions, to take certain decisions, possibly to hire and fire people, to allocate money, and to make appointments. This type of power is often called "authority" because it is official and legitimate.
- *Expert Power:*
  The possession of knowledge or experience or skills can gain you the respect of others, allowing you to influence them. This type of power confers another sort of authority, that of the expert, as when we say "She speaks with authority" and mean that she knows what she is talking about. Expert power is unusual because the power is effectively given to you by the very people over whom you are going to use it. It is no use your proclaiming yourself to be a great expert if no one believes you. The great bores are the self-proclaimed experts who drone on without any noticeable influence on those listening, unless it be to send them to sleep.

Resource power, position power, expert power—the differences are important. In the past, in organizations, it was resource power that counted. He who paid the piper always called the tune. As time went on and organizations became bigger and more formal, position power was the one that mattered. The marketing director could control the work—and much of the life—of the regional sales rep, the head teacher was effectively judge and master of the junior teacher, even of the department head as well. More recently, as democratic values reach into our organizations, it is the kind of authority that is *earned,* expert power, that counts more and more. The teacher in the classroom may have all the formal authority of his or her position, but without the personal authority that comes from experience, personality, and expertise, it may be hard to get the kids to learn, let alone behave.

> "Why shouldn't I smoke if I want to?" said my teenage son.
>
> "Because . . ." I said, launching into a reasoned argument on the dangers to health, and on the offense it gave to nonsmokers.
>
> "I don't think your data are quite correct. . . ." He began to deploy more statistics, his right to choose his own health, his permission from everyone else in the room to smoke if he wanted. . . . My credibility as an expert was vanishing!
>
> "As your father—" I started again, reaching back to my position power in the family.
>
> "Oh, come on, dad, don't be so Victorian," he laughed, killing the hope that I still had some authority in that role.
>
> "Well," I said, falling back on resource power as a last resort, "suppose I make a deal? No smoking and $500 when you are twenty-one."
>
> "Now you're talking," he said, "but the numbers are too small."
>
> It is harder than I thought to be a father in a democratic family.

Most bosses behave in much the same way as I did with my son. Expert power is the most acceptable way of influencing people because they have given you the power themselves, the credibility you are now using to change their ways or their thinking. As a writer, I have only expert power. If you want to throw this book away there is nothing I can do to stop you. On the other hand, if you read it and agree with any of it, you will not resent my changing the way you think, but may be, perhaps, modestly grateful for my exercise of influence.

Everybody would like it to be that way. Persuasion is the most pleasant form of influence. But when it fails, why then, formal authority is brought in: "Because I say so," says the beleaguered parent; "Well, these are my instructions, and that is final," says the embattled manager. Fine—until the troops mutiny or, more usually, quietly ignore the instructions. More authority (the boss's boss) is brought in and, ultimately, it comes to a question of resources, "unless you—" or "if you—"

John was delighted. He had been pulled out of the sales force to be the first distribution coordinator, a new job that had been created following a consultant's report. He would act as a liaison between sales and production, making sure that the product runs matched the sales requirements without stockpiling or running out. It was clearly an important job. He needed his authority to be recognized throughout the organization, for people to realize that he was now in charge of this operation. He started by making sure that he got a decent office near the sales department, with entrance only via his secretary (very important!), had special internal letterheads printed, and bought himself two new business suits. No one was impressed. "Who does he think he is?" "Pity he doesn't do the job instead of feathering his little nest." "He isn't going to coordinate much if we can't see him."

By trying to boost the outward signs of his position power, John had given away what little expert power he had.

If John was going to have any impact on the organization he was going to have to rely on *negative power.* Even the humblest of us can all stop something, even if we cannot start anything. Watch the conductor on a London bus turn passengers away on a wet night with seats to spare. "Sorry, no room." It is an illusion of power, much needed by those who feel powerless or frustrated.

I was once dignified with the grand title of Assistant Coordinator, Regional Marketing, Mediterranean Region, Excluding France. It sounded important, but in fact I was merely a post office, receiving

> reports and requests from the various countries around the Mediterranean (France was accepted as being a law unto itself) and making sure that they reached the right departments with any necessary background notes. I was bored—angry that there was so little scope for what I thought were my talents. I spent a lot of the day looking out of the window, speculating on the lives of the people walking below.
>
> One day, a proposal came in from our Italian company for a refinery in the Bay of Naples. What an awful idea, I thought, but knowing full well that it would probably go through because the economics were too tempting.
>
> I remember picking up the whole pile of papers and dropping them quite deliberately in the trash bin. Four weeks later, more copies arrived, this time with extra copies for my boss and for other departments. They got their refinery. No one knew what I had done with the original letter. But for four weeks I had blocked that eyesore in the bay. I hugged myself, secretly. I had some negative power, at least.

Gatekeepers who turn up late, secretaries who lose files, drivers who lose their way, even the lowliest can cause delay, if not catastrophe. Higher up, there are people expert in the use of committees to block things, who can find a clause somewhere in some manual prohibiting something, who can fail to arrange a meeting until it is too late. Frustrated bureaucrats are not impotent, they all have the opportunity to use their negative power somehow.

Keep people stretched, give them as much responsibility as they can handle, allow them discretion and the space to make decisions, and they will feel no need to use their negative power; they will have plenty of the positive kind. The fewer the procedures, the flatter the hierarchy, the more open the communications, the less the opportunity for blocking tactics. Flat, busy, open organizations are always less prone to this organizational disease of negative power.

Politics is the attempt to accumulate more resource and position power in order to increase one's influence in the organization. That need not always be a purely selfish thing to do—most of us believe that if we had more influence we could make things work better, but, just sometimes, we want the power, even if it's mostly negative power, to protect our own backs.

Resources and positions and roles are, however, fragile things—they can disappear or be taken from you overnight. Spare an occasional thought for the man who is CEO on Friday and retired CEO on Monday, *sans* office, *sans* secretary, *sans* car, *sans* everything that was a symbol of his position. Now an individual—just a name, not a title—his influence will depend only on his acknowledged skill and experience, on his expertise. In the end expert power is the power base that lasts, because only you yourself can destroy it, or fail to renew it. It is the sort of power that is least resented or opposed, because it is granted to you by a consensus of those over whom you exercise it, and because they are still free to ignore it. It is the power base that is most efficient, because if people agree with you, they will go along with your wishes without further checks, controls, or kicks.

We cannot, however, all be acknowledged experts in all our jobs. Most of us have to make do with what resources and positions we have to get the things done that we want done. It makes sense, then, to have friends in the right places (increasing position power), to build alliances with other departments (more resources), to collect as much information as you can (information is a resource), and to trim proposals to what is likely to be acceptable (a compromise attracts less negative power). In other words, we have to play politics. So do it, but know what you are doing, because, carried to extremes, it can be mischievous.

Andrew Pettigrew once listed in *Personnel Review* the devices a line manager in a big business can use to fend off a report by a specialist that makes unpopular recommendations:

1. Straight rejection—the specialist and the report are dismissed without further discussion. This needs a lot of resource and position power, and a big dollop of self-assurance.

2. "Bottom drawer it"—the report is praised but nothing is done about it. The specialist, content with the praise, may not press for action.

3. Mobilizing political support—the executive calls on support from colleagues who have similar interests.

4. The nitty-gritty tactic—minor objections are raised to discredit and delay the full report.

5. "But in the future . . ."—the report is OK today but will not work in tomorrow's conditions—therefore it is not worth implementing.
6. The emotional tactic—"How can you do this to me?" or ". . . to my colleagues?"
7. The invisible man tactic—the line manager is never available for discussion about the report.
8. "Further investigation is required"—the report is sent back for more work.
9. The scapegoat—someone else (say, head office) won't like it.
10. Deflection—the line manager directs attention to the points where he has sufficient knowledge to contradict the specialist—and so discredit the report.

These are not ten commandments, but ten ways to abuse your position power.

THE NECESSITY OF COMPROMISE

Few people have power enough to do everything they want to do. Perhaps that is just as well, because power does tend to corrupt. If anything is to happen, compromises have to be made. Sticking to the rules or to one's principles can be a form of negative power. There is a morality in compromise, if the result is progress.

SOME QUESTIONS FOR THINKING AND TALKING ABOUT

Getting organized means being aware of what your power bases are and how, in particular, your expert power can be increased.

1. List some examples of your own power.
   a. What resources do you control—for example, budgets, information?
   b. What decisions does your position entitle you to make—for example, money, people?

c. What are you thought by others to be expert in?
d. Only your expert power can be increased by your own efforts. How can you do this—for example, courses, participation in meetings, help from colleagues?
2. List some examples of negative power used against you.
a. Why was it used? Fear, jealousy, or because you were wrong?
b. How could you have prevented its use? More involvement of other parties, better explanations, or a compromise?
3. Whom do you most admire in the organization?
a. What power bases does he or she rely on?
b. What political strategies, alliances, and so on does he or she use? Can you do likewise?

"I recall a recent Foreign Secretary talking to a group of bishops about the realities of power. 'I was alone in the Foreign Office in August,' he said. 'My senior colleagues were away on holiday. I received a telegram from our Ambassador in Tehran, where the Shah was in his last months of power. *Send riot shields for the Shah's police,* it said. I rang the Ambassador. No way could I agree, I said, to give equipment to the Shah's police—it is against all our principles to support the Shah's use of force. If you don't, said the Ambassador, he will have to use his tanks. If you send equipment for his police you may save the citizens of Tehran from being murdered in their streets. I sent the riot shields. If you want things to happen sensibly you sometimes have to compromise your principles.'

Or change some of your priorities."

13 Teams and Captains

It was another of those English summers. Headlines every second week proclaiming "England Collapses" or "Defeat Inevitable." A stranger would have thought that another world war was in progress, but it was only an international cricket match. I am no cricket expert, but it puzzles me how England selectors with eleven places to fill and the whole of English youth to choose from can still find themselves short of a spin bowler or an opening batsman. They cannot even find a captain who can direct his men on the field and also represent them, with style and good humor, to the press and the rest of the world.

Teams are a part of English life. Most boys, and many a girl, have their favorite football team, every youngster has a pet pop group. A friend made a lifetime dream come true when he was able to collect a team of his friends to play his village at cricket. The village won but that was not the point—it was, he said, the wonderful team spirit the occasion aroused.

How odd, then, that the English so seldom apply to their organizations what they all (except for their cricket selectors) understand so well about teams in sport. I once, jokingly and ironically, said that a "rowing eight" was the only really true English team—eight people going backwards without speaking to each other, steered by the one person who can't row! I was gently reprimanded. They can only do this wondrous thing, I was told, because they know and trust each other so well that they don't need to speak and can put their whole energy into pulling the oars, confident that the little cox is steering them in the right direction.

They were right, of course. And what they, and all of us, know about teams in sport applies just as much to teams in organizations.

There are four crucial points to remember about teams:

- Teams are collections of differences.
- Teams are not committees.
- Teams have a life of their own.
- Teams can become too cozy.

TEAMS ARE COLLECTIONS OF DIFFERENCES

No one in their right mind would put eleven bowlers in a cricket team, or try to make up a football team out of eleven goalkeepers. The point seems so obvious that it is trivial, yet organizations are still prone to what has been called the Apollo syndrome—they think that a team of the brightest people will automatically outperform any other. It doesn't. A team must contain all the different technical skills required to do the task. Less obviously, perhaps, it also needs a range of different personalities, or people with different kinds of priorities.

Meredith Belbin, a British researcher, has a widely accepted list of eight roles that are all needed in a good team.

The Chairperson. The one with the job of picking the people, listening to them and encouraging them, and focusing and coordinating the effort. Someone in this role would rather be called *disciplined, focused,* and *balanced* than expert or creative.

The Shaper. The task leader, outgoing and forceful; someone whose strength lies in personal drive and passion for the task. Shapers are needed as the spur for action but can be impatient.

The Plant. The source of original ideas and proposals, the Plant is the most creative and intelligent member of the team but can be careless of details. Plants need to be drawn out to give their best.

The Monitor Evaluator. The one who does the checking and points out the flaws in the argument, the Monitor Evaluator is better at analysis than creativity.

The Resource Investigator. The liaison person who keeps the team in touch with the world around it. People who gravitate to this role tend to be popular and extroverted.

The Company Worker. The practical organizer and administrator who turns ideas into timetables for action.

The Team Worker. Likeable and popular, the team worker keeps everybody going by encouragement and understanding and support.

The Finisher. Without the Finisher the team might never meet its deadlines. The Finisher's relentless follow-through is important but not always popular.

I cannot remember eight types, let alone the eleven or fifteen people required in some teams. Four are enough for me. A team always needs among its members people who will fill these parts: the Captain, the Administrator, the Driver who will push the task through, and the Expert, the one with the knowledge and ideas.

In other words, choose the people who need to get the job done technically, but then make sure that among them there are those who will fill these other important parts. (It is, incidentally, not a coincidence that the four main parts in a team bear a close similarity to the four gods in Chapter Sixteen.) No one, in sport, selects the top eleven or fifteen players—they also have to select those who are able to play in certain positions. What is true on the sports field is crucial in an organization; the four key roles have to be filled, somehow, if the team is to make the best use of all its skills. It may even be that the Captain, or the Administrator, would not be in the team as an ordinary player, but is needed solely to provide essential skills as Captain or Administrator. After all, in sport, there are such things as nonplaying Captains.

It was, they told me, a wonderful family—but quite hopeless. I could see what they meant when I got there. There was a passionate argument going on, which everyone seemed to be enjoying immensely. One teenager was immersed in a computer, writing a program to make up crossword puzzles, I was told; another, much younger, was making wine out of nettles, with much anguish. The mother was one of those arguing—something about whether or not Poland was a great country or a disaster. No one took any notice of our arrival. We had been asked to lunch but no lunch was visible.

"Oh—so sorry, didn't see you there—come in—meet Angus, and Angela, and Anthony and, I can't remember your name, but she's Anthony's friend, and do sit down, there or wherever, it doesn't matter—and yes, food, you'll want some, I suppose, we all will—what shall we have? Angus, could you help? No, you sit down and make yourselves at home—lovely to see you, just lovely. . . ."

She enveloped us all in her warmth, we were glad to be there, but it was another two hours before lunch, of a sort, appeared.

The family, I realized, had Experts galore, a Captain, too, who held them all together in her enveloping warmth, but they needed an Administrator—and a Driver, too, if they were ever going to get enough to eat. Why bother, they would have said, a family does not have to be a team. Quite so. As long as it's not a family business.

TEAMS ARE NOT COMMITTEES

A camel, the saying goes, is a horse designed by a committee, which is a polite way of saying that most committees end up with a compromise. That is OK because that is what committees are for—to find an acceptable working compromise. Teams, however, are there to win. The two must not be confused.

Teams are collections of individuals gathered together because their talents are needed to perform a task or to solve a problem. If the team wins, all those in it win. If the team loses, they all lose. There is a common purpose, and the sense of camaraderie that should go with a common purpose. This is true whether the collection of individuals is a project task force or Unit 6 on the production floor.

Committees are collections of *representatives* gathered together because they all have an interest in a particular problem or issue. The job of the committee is to find a solution that is acceptable to all. Almost inevitably that means a compromise. Compromises are necessary in life if anything is to happen, but they do not feel exciting. Few people enjoy committees, but they do have their place in organizations.

It is the instinct of any good chairperson to turn a committee into a team by making their joint task more important to them, more exciting to them as individuals, than the interests or groups they are supposed to represent. It is a tactic that, in organizations, can boomerang when the representatives return from their new team to find that their home bases are not as enthusiastic as they are about their new tasks and are not prepared to support them. If this happens the team solution is disowned and nothing happens. The committee should have been left as it was, unexciting though it might have been, because it was only a meeting of representatives.

Teams should never be turned into committees. Teams are made up of individuals whose first loyalty is to the team. Treat these individuals as representatives and their loyalty becomes divided, their commitment confused, and their duty uncertain. Teams do not have agendas or minutes, except in a very abbreviated form, they prefer informal get-togethers to structured meetings, and they have leaders, not chairpersons, first names, not titles.

TEAMS HAVE A LIFE OF THEIR OWN

Teams, like human beings, are born, grow up, and grow old. You can watch them *forming,* creating their own identity, finding out who each individual is and what part they might play, choosing a name or a symbol. For many teams there is then a kind of adolescence, a time of *storming,* when individuals begin to assert themselves to challenge the original shape or purpose of the team. The original identity, the first allocation of parts, was wrong, people say, we were too new, too accepting, too unsure of ourselves. Now we know. After the storming comes the *norming,* when the team begins to settle down to a new way of working, when the Captain, the Administrator, the Driver, the Expert, and the other types, begin to make their contributions. Lastly, there is the time of full maturity when the team can really *perform.*

These stages of growth—forming, storming, norming, and performing—seem to be a necessary part of any team's life. To neglect them, to insist on immediate performance without any time to get to know each other, or to work out whose job it is to do what, will often result in a sort of delayed adolescence when the group starts to disintegrate. Then the whole process of growing up as a team has to start all over again.

Without the chance to grow up and grow together as a temporary family, a team will not be able to develop the kind of trust that good rowing eights have—the trust that allows you to do your thing, confident that the rest are doing theirs, the trust that stops you competing with the other members for individual glory, the trust that reassures you that when you pass the ball there will be someone there to catch it. Teams need trust to work efficiently; they need time to build that trust, time to grow up.

> They were five friends, in their late teens, all contemporary musicians. It was natural that as soon as they left school they should form themselves into a proper band, compose their own songs, do some gigs, perhaps, who knows, get signed up to make a record or two, even an album.
>
> It was fun. Then it became serious. They were spotted by a talent scout at a gig. He found the finance to hire a studio and a producer to put together a demo tape.
>
> Trevor began to feel uneasy. He talked to Rod, who talked to Mike and Bill. The problem was Charlie, their singer. He wasn't, if they were frank about it, good enough, not good enough for the real thing now they were on the edge of it. He wasn't good enough as a singer, nor as the front man of the band. Trevor, they all knew in their hearts, would do it better, far better. But Charlie was their friend, they had known him all their young lives, they had a responsibility to him.
>
> The dilemma ached like a sore tooth. The old camaraderie and trust was gone. There was a falseness in the air, and lots of silences. The band was not working properly any more.
>
> That night they bit the bullet. They took Charlie out to an Indian restaurant and told him. He sort of knew already, they felt. It wasn't nice, but it was better in the end to be honest and open, better for the band, certainly; better, they hoped, for Charlie.

> "Teams aren't easy, Dad," Trevor said that night to his father, "but I think we've grown up a bit tonight, and I think we'll play better tomorrow."

Storming can be just as painful even when it's quiet. Without it, however, and the pain that goes with it sometimes, there will not be the trust that every team needs to be able to pull together without talking, like a good crew.

TEAMS CAN BECOME TOO COZY

Close teams can become closed teams. *Groupthink,* it is called, when groups develop a life and a view of their own, and become blind and deaf to anyone or anything else. The desire to be a close-knit little family can sometimes go too far.

"How could we have been so stupid?" asked President Kennedy, after he and a group of close advisers had blundered into the decision to invade Cuba in the Bay of Pigs—a disastrous adventure. Stupidity was certainly not the explanation. The group that made the decision was one of the greatest collections of intellectual talent in the history of American government. It was groupthink. Groupthink occurs when a group is so close that nothing must be allowed to upset the harmony of the team. Outsiders, and outside views, are unwelcome. Doubts or questions feel like disloyalty and are stifled. The team builds up a false sense of self-confidence, sure that its previous success makes it almost invincible, that it must be right, that everyone else is wrong, or feeble, or just jealous.

Governments can get this way after too long in office. Generals, notoriously, train for the last war but not the next. Boards of companies, promoting their own shadows and recruiting friends as outside directors, can go this way. Family businesses are particularly prone to it because no one wants to break up a family as well as a team. Any organization that keeps the same people in the same places for years is in danger of it—some schools, for example, or small businesses that do not grow.

The cure for groupthink is to encourage a climate of open inquiry and debate, using outsiders as the catalysts. Good teams have critical coaches who do not let them become complacent. Good teams watch videotapes of their matches and criticize their own performances. Outside directors, consultants, and independent advisers are the equivalent of coaches and video recorders for organizations. They should be used.

> I was listening in, as a researcher and observer, to the board debating its five-year strategy. The company ran a string of photographic laboratories, processing film for a range of chemists and photographic stores.
>
> Over coffee one of the directors had been telling me of a magazine article predicting that before very long film processing would be completely automatic, with strips of film being dropped into a black box in the retail outlet and the final prints emerging at the bottom—all done, on the spot, in fifteen minutes.
>
> After coffee the meeting resumed. The board discussed the proposed expansion and extension of their laboratory network. No mention was made of the magazine article.
>
> "Why didn't you discuss it?" I asked afterward.
>
> "It wasn't on the agenda," he said, "and, anyway, it's just an idea. It hasn't happened yet, no need to worry our heads about it now."
>
> They were a great team—with their heads in the sand.

Teams are here to stay. We cannot avoid them. Most of life is now too complicated to be dealt with by one woman or one man on their own. A good team is a great place to be, exciting, stimulating, supportive, successful. A bad team is horrible, a sort of human prison. We can make teams good if we understand them—they seldom happen that way by chance.

SOME QUESTIONS FOR THINKING AND TALKING ABOUT

Getting organized requires that we take teams seriously.

1. List all the groups you belong to and the principal meetings you attend.

   a. Which are run as teams and which as committees?
   b. Have they got them right, or are there committees that should be teams, or vice versa? How could they be changed?
2. List the members of the teams to which you belong.
   a. Which of them is Captain, Administrator, Driver, Expert?
   b. Have the right people got the right parts?
3. Take a major problem you think needs tackling in your area, one that is not necessarily your direct responsibility.
   a. Pick your ideal team from all the people you know.
   b. How could you help the team to develop if you were in charge?

> “‘I can't imagine why that couple are married,’ I said. ‘They seem to disagree on almost everything—from politics through religion to bringing up their children.’
>
> ‘I think you're missing something,’ my wife said. ‘They have a lot in common underneath, the same love of countryside and family, the same priorities for their home and their own lives, the same basic beliefs in work and honesty and straight dealing. What you hear and see is only the froth on top of something sure and deep that has been, for them, twenty-six years of shared history.’
>
> ‘Well, I still think that oil and water don't mix and don't make for a true relationship.’
>
> ‘No, but oil and *petrol* do mix because, underneath, they are the same. Life would be very boring if we all agreed with each other all the time. What makes a marriage great is the trust and confidence that allows one to argue about the little things, knowing that one agrees about the big things.’
>
> It works for groups, too, I thought.”

14 Outward and Visible Signs

I grew up in a rectory. The time came, therefore, when I was prepared for confirmation. That preparation involved something called the catechism: "an instruction," said the old prayer book, "to be learned of every person before he be brought to be confirmed by the Bishop." I was not, I fear, a very diligent student; I have forgotten most of it. I remember, however, one splendid phrase, "an outward and visible sign of an inward and spiritual grace." The phrase has stuck with me over the years, reminding me that it is no good just having all sorts of good intentions, you have also got to give some outward and visible sign of those good feelings. I am forever intending to write long letters to distant friends and relatives. However, the intentions do me, and them, no good unless there is some outward and visible sign of them, like a letter in an envelope with a stamp and an address.

It also works in reverse. You can tell a lot about the inward goings-on from the outward and visible signs. In fact, you have to if that is all the evidence you have to go on. There is, however, a lot of room for mistakes because there is no sure guarantee that just because a house has a pub sign outside it, there is going to be beer available within. Indeed, in Street—a town in Somerset—there used to be a nonalcoholic pub. I can also still recall my disappointment, as a young Irishman arriving in England, at finding that a Free House sign hanging outside a pub did not mean that all drinks were free, but only that the pub was not tied to a particular brewer.

When you think about it, we spend much of our time making assumptions about what's inside someone, or something, on the basis of very scanty information on the outside. When looking for a new house, half the time I know that I need not bother to go inside—everything I see outside tells me that it is not going to be right. I felt this once when I arrived at the house of some friends to find just a big wall onto the street with a few tiny slits for windows and a tiny door in the middle. Not for me, this sort of house, I thought, I want space and light and greenery. But they were expecting me, so I pressed the bell. The door was opened and I stepped into a courtyard with a lawn running down to a stream, the house being built down two sides of the courtyard. I could not have been more wrong. "Ah," they said, when I told them of my surprise, "that is deliberate; no one thinks there is a proper house here, it keeps the burglars away." In this case my friends knew and liked the impression their outward appearance gave to the visitor. Not all of our organizations are so clever.

On one course that I run for part-time management students in their early thirties, they are required, as a small group of five or six, to spend a day in one another's organizations discovering what sort of places they are, what customs, values, and styles prevail, what theories of management they seem to rely on. As part of the exercise I now ask them to take photographs of the outside of the building, of the entrance and the reception area, of some of the offices and workplaces. They are then asked to present these pictures on a screen in front of the whole class, without identifying the organization or saying anything about it. The rest of the class is then asked to predict the culture and the style of the organization, to guess, in fact, the inward workings from the outward appearance. It is remarkable how often they get it right.

One group of students based their whole analysis of the organization's problems around photographs of the windows in the building. The first photograph showed the building two years earlier. It was a large brick building that had originally been a mill. Now it was used as the headquarters of a papermaking firm and was all offices. The first floor had new, much larger windows, with one double one on the corner. It was not hard to guess where the directors sat and where the chairman sat. The building, however, looked seedy. There were weeds in the driveway and the paintwork badly needed attention.

In the later photographs, the whole building had been fixed up. There was a new and imposing entrance gate and a penthouse floor with enormous windows. The firm had been taken over, the old chairman eased out, and his office made into a drawing office. The other offices on the first floor were also, now, open-plan accounting offices, signaled by Venetian blinds on the windows instead of flowered curtains. The new regime was installed on top where a small flat nestled next door to the CEO's office—living space for the new chairman on his very occasional visits. It was all an outward and visible sign of an internal revolution.

Strangely, although we all know that we make huge assumptions on the basis of a few early images, organizations pay very little heed to first impressions. Reception areas can be dark and gloomy, or even nonexistent. I used to try in vain to find the proper way into a certain primary school, ending up, as often as not, in the kitchen near the parking lot. One television company has contracted out its reception to a security firm, making one wonder what sort of people are running its studios. Others combine their receptionist with their telephone operator, which sounds efficient but usually means that either the visitor or the telephone caller has to be kept waiting, arousing suspicions that this organization is not too concerned about the convenience of its customers. Telephones, generally, are a neglected area and yet, for most people, they are the first contact they will have with the organization. There is nothing more frustrating than to have to wait for twenty rings and then have a bored voice telling you that they are putting you through—often to a complete silence. How many chief executives, I sometimes wonder, ever try to telephone their own offices? They might be surprised, unpleasantly surprised!

There is a lot of evidence that working in comfortable and even beautiful places is good for efficiency. Only recently have architects and doctors jointly recognized that there is something called *office-sickness*—a psychological outcome of working in noisy, cramped, or unventilated buildings, of feeling imprisoned, hemmed in, or just depressed by miles of pale green corridors. Many people could have told the architects years ago that the outward and visible signs affect one's inward and, yes, spiritual grace. I once worked in a tall office building, so uniform throughout that one had to look at the numbers on the office doors in the long windowless corridors to know if one was on the right level or in the correct wing. It was a modern building, but the general feeling was that the only good view of it was the view from inside looking out. My soul shrank within me every morning when I entered that building and like everyone else I left on the dot at 5:20 P.M., the end of the official day. I found my work cheerless when, thinking about it, it could have been quite an exciting job.

Things are changing. British Airways has built a new head office outside London that has its own street running through the middle, a street with restaurants and shops for the staff, with little and big buildings off it, to give the feeling of a village in a city—not a tower or a prison. It is a famous building, much photographed, although hard to photograph because it is not really one building. It must be fun to work in a place designed to be fun. They say it is. Other businesses are imitating British Airways. The outward and visible bits do not just give clues to what is inside, they affect it.

What goes for organizations works for people, too. What we look like provides clues, whether true or false, to what we are inside. We all act on these clues, jumping, sometimes too fast, to conclusions, relying on stereotypes; "professors are absent-minded," "blondes are dumb," "older men don't change," "accountants are boring," "Scotsmen are tight-fisted." We all know enough exceptions to prove that these particular rules are false but we still have some of our own. My mother-in-law would never trust a man who wore brown shoes with a blue suit, particularly if they were suede. This was not a matter of taste, she really believed it indicated a character flaw, an outward and physical sign of a lack of inward grace.

Society, of course, uses outward and visible signs to indicate the kinds of authority people carry. Policemen look like policemen and are intended to do so, which means that plainclothes policemen are also intended to be invisible, the better to carry out their undercover work. Do presidential bodyguards, I wonder, intend to be so obvious, with suits that bulge under the armpits, and crew-cut hair. Their outward and visible signs can hardly be missed, but perhaps they are not meant to be. Priests dress like priests to give people the permission to use them as priests, so that everyone can know who they are. Novels and plays are built around plots that use visual imagery to confuse, as when master and servant switch their clothes, or the escaped prisoner puts on a clerical collar.

We do it ourselves, all the time. The jeans and open-necked shirt are meant to indicate an informal attitude. "We don't wear ties here, just be comfortable." It can of course be horribly confusing to newcomers, unsure of whether they are talking to the chairperson or the janitor. I sometimes use clothes quite deliberately to give a message that I'm different; jeans and sweater with a group of bankers, suit and tie with some creative designers. Most people, however, adopt a uniform: the dark suit, the tailored coat and skirt, the all-black apparel of the teenager, the dinner jacket or the morning suit for formal occasions. These uniforms, of course, also confuse. They tell people what tribe you belong to, but they do not give much information about your individual differences. People can hide behind uniforms, and often do. Firms, therefore, that insist, Japanese-style, on white coats for everyone are saying two things. They are saying that status is not too important around here—the message they want to convey, but they also appear to be saying that individuality is not too much desired either.

> I once was asked to talk to a group of managers at the staff college of one of the large banks. It was a very formal evening. Everyone was in suits, in rows, in upright chairs. They all wore their names and titles on their lapels. After I had spoken the session was chaired, very formally, by the head of college. I was placed for dinner at the top table between the head and his deputy. I never felt that I got close to the student managers or to their problems. I mentioned this, afterwards, to the head and said

that, in my view, such formality did not encourage frank discussion or any real learning, it was all just a kind of ritual.

Next time I went everything was different. This lot of managers were in casual dress. We sat in a large circle of armchairs and sofas. Drinks were available. Supper was a buffet affair. It was all very informal and I enjoyed it immensely. I was staggered by the change.

"Is it always like this now?" I asked one of the young managers.

"Oh, no," he said, "just today. Look!" And he showed me a paper pinned on the bulletin board, headed "Orders for the Day."

"In conformity with the wishes of our speaker tonight," it read, "dress will be informal, the session will be held in the Reading Room, not the Lecture Theater, where drinks and supper will also be available. First names are to be used. These orders apply to this session only."

"You see," he said, "it's all for you."

Outward and visible signs do not always mean what they say.

It is not only clothes that provide the clues. We have a whole armory of tones of voice, expressions, ways of standing, glances of eye or smiles of lips. We use these to indicate on the outside the way we are feeling on the inside. Sometimes we do not know that we are doing it and we can give away more than we mean to. "Do you really like him?" my daughter asked me, of her new friend. "Yes, very much," I replied, but it was the four-second pause before my answer which, to her mind, gave the lie to my words. "I can see you don't," she said.

Sometimes we deliberately give out false signs. "Oozing charm from every pore," the salesman can con some people that he really believes what he is saying. Some people spend most of their time keeping up appearances. One wonders why. It may be to avoid causing embarrassment, as when we feign composure after a bereavement, or do not want to worry others with an illness or our poverty. Too often, however, it is done in an attempt to persuade people that our inside selves are different from what they really are. There is the executive who feigns busyness, picking up the phone as soon as you enter the room, then putting it down, as if to say, "This can wait—but not for too long." At the other extreme, there is the clear-desk fanatic, nothing visible but all in the bottom drawer or in the secretary's pending tray. Are they wise to try to live a lie? Most of the time, those close to them are not deceived.

The average person, however, does not give out false clues, he or she gives no clues at all. We think that our inner feelings and intentions speak for themselves. "No, of course I wanted you to be involved"—well, why then did he not receive copies of the correspondence? "Don't be silly. I have the greatest respect for you and I think your work is consistently good"—why, then, is this the first time that you have told her? "I'm really disappointed that I did not get the chance to go on one of the new courses"—but did you mention to anyone that you wanted to?

My boss had the annoying habit of assuming that I knew everything that was going on in his mind. He would not, therefore, bother to fill me in on what he was thinking about but would suddenly inquire, "Will Jim be good enough for it, do you think?"—assuming that I knew what "it" was. In a wife such an assumption of understanding may be touching; in a boss, it is irritating. Mental telepathy is not, I find, a reliable means of communication in most organizations. One's inward intentions need outward signs.

It is not part of my intention to recommend that organizations, or individuals, should pretend to be what they are not; that would be to live a lie. Both should be what they seem to be. They would be wise, however, to examine whether what they seem to be is what they really are—whether those outward and visible signs tell the story they should be telling. If the story is slightly better than the truth, then the truth should be brought in line. If, as so often happens, the signs only tell part of the story, then the signs need adjustment.

SOME QUESTIONS FOR THINKING AND TALKING ABOUT

Getting organized requires that you and your organization are seen to be what you really are.

1. Look at your organization, at its appearance, at the way it receives visitors, or callers, or customers. Try phoning in.
   a. What messages does it give out?

   b. What needs changing or improving?
2. Look at yourself.
   a. What aspects of your character or talents seem to go unnoticed or unappreciated?
   b. What signs have you given to others of these things?
   c. What could you do differently?
3. Talk to your colleagues. Ask them to pick out one habit of yours, or one clue in your appearance, behavior, or surroundings, that is most symbolic of you. Do you believe them?

> “It annoys me—so many of the pictures hanging in our house seem to be slightly crooked, knocked by a passing shoulder, perhaps, or blown off center by the wind. I spend quite a lot of my time fiddling with them, putting them straight on their cords. ‘Sometimes,’ says my wife, ‘I think that you only look at the frames of those pictures, not at what’s inside the frames.’
>
> Maybe she’s right. I know people like that in organizations—obsessed by the *way* things are done more than by *what* things are done.”

15 Tribes and Their Ways

Long ago I fell in love. We decided to get married. We asked, or rather told, her parents and mine. We arranged the ceremony. And that, we thought, was that. We would live happily or semi-happily ever after, having a family no doubt, building a home, making a double life for ourselves. What I had not realized was that behind her, and behind me, was a whole tribe of family, relations, friends—a tribe that, willy-nilly, I was joining, just as she was joining my tribe. The two tribes were very different—as became clear at the wedding ceremony—with their own traditions, values, and customs. One tribe liked to drink, the other did not, one tribe was army, the other tribe was churchy, one was Irish, one was English, one was overpolite, one was jocularly abusive. I found that I had chosen a wife—but married a tribe. It has been, shall we say, interesting!

Organizations, too, are tribes, or sometimes collections of tribes, tribes that can be very different in the way they behave, in their assumptions and their traditions. We should not be surprised. A church is not likely to be the same as a factory, nor a bank run like a supermarket, nor a school like either. You will find, in fact, that every organization is probably different, just as every family is different.

Is there then nothing that we can say about organizations in general? Is there nothing that they have in common? They are, after all, all made up of people, and people, although individuals, all have some things in common. I now believe that it is a compromise between being unique and being the same. Every organization indeed is different but is still a blend of the same four tribes. The basic ingredients of any organization, in other words, can be described, but they will always be put together in different proportions in different situations. It will help to understand your organization if you understand the four tribes that make it up. It is likely that there will be only one tribe occupying your part of the organization, but remember there may be other tribes in other parts. As I discovered in marriage, you need to know what tribe you are joining; life will be more comfortable and effective if you share common values and ways.

The bigger the organization, the more tribes you will find. "Sales" will be one and so will "accounting," "the women in X division" and "the men in division Y," all will have a distinct tribal feeling about them. Merge, or try to merge, two organizations and the tribal loyalties come out, with each tribe sure that their way is best. Sometimes it can seem to the newcomer that there is a different tribe on every floor—and, indeed, there often may be. It is comforting then to realize that each tribe has to belong to one of only four different types.

> "Those ways won't do around here," he said. "You'll have to forget all that free and easy stuff now you're in the real world."
>
> Jill had joined the production team of the Portsmouth plant of the company she worked for after two years' work at the laboratory in Cambridge. She had joined the company straight after her degree and had found the product development work fascinating, a sort of practical extension of her university course. She and two others had spent the two years working on one product. Their time was their own. They worked long hours but largely at their own discretion, taking time off for meals or for meetings, or even to attend the occasional seminar in the university when it seemed appropriate. They met with their boss every second Tuesday to discuss progress.

> Now, in Portsmouth, Jill was supervising a small production unit doing trials on her product. Life in the factory, she found, was different. Timekeeping was essential, she had to be there when the others were there. Forms had to be filled in, disciplines kept, rules observed. There were obvious layers of authority and her boss was always around.
>
> "I suppose it's right," she said, "but it's very different from Cambridge."

Each tribe has a name—there's the club tribe, the role tribe, the task tribe, and the person tribe—and a symbol or a picture to represent it. Each tribe subscribes to a central *organizational idea*—beliefs about the best way to organize things and get something done, about the right way to treat people and the right way to behave. The four tribes have four very different organizational ideas; each works well in certain circumstances, each set of beliefs is good, in its place. What set of beliefs suits you best? Which tribe do you want to join? Read on to find out.

THE CLUB TRIBE

The best picture to illustrate this kind of organization is a spider's web, because the key to the whole organization sits in the center, surrounded by ever-widening circles of intimates and influence. The closer you are to the spider, the more influence you have. There are other lines in the web—the lines of responsibility, the functions of the organization, stretching out from the center—but the intimacy circles are the important ones, because this organization works like a club, a club built around its leader.

The organizational idea is that the organization is there as an extension of the person at the head, often the founder. If the spiders could do everything personally, they would. It is because they can't that there has to be an organization at all. So the organization should simply be an extension of themselves, acting on their behalf, a club of like-minded people.

That can sound like a dictatorship, and some club organizations are dictatorships of the owner or founder. However, at their best, club tribes are based on trust and communicate by a sort of telepathy, with everyone knowing everyone else's mind. They are very personal places, for the

THE CLUB TRIBE

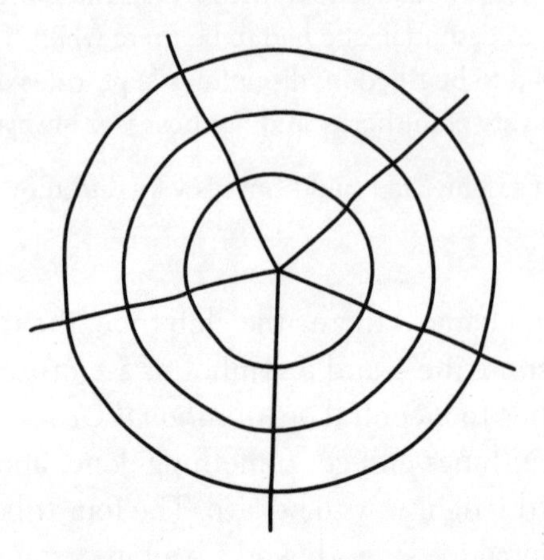

spiders preserve their freedom to maneuver by writing little down, preferring to talk to people, to sense their reactions and infect them with their own enthusiasms and passions. If there are memoranda or minutes of meetings, they go from Gill to Joe or, more often, from one set of initials to another set of initials, rather than from job title to job title.

These types of organization, therefore, are rich in personality. They abound with almost mythic stories and folklore from the past and can be very exciting places to work, if you belong to the club and share the values and beliefs of the spider. Their great strength is in their ability to respond immediately and intuitively to opportunities or crises because of the very short lines of communication and because of the centralization of power. Their danger lies in the dominance of the character of the central figure. Without a spider, the web is dead. If the spider is weak, corrupt, inept, or picks the wrong people, the organization is also weak, corrupt, inept, and badly staffed. Finding a new spider becomes a critical decision.

These organizations thrive where personality and speed of response are critical, in new business situations, in deals and brokerage transactions, in the artistic and theatrical worlds, in politics, guerrilla warfare, and crisis situations, provided always that the leader is good (they talk of leaders rather than managers in these places). They are a convenient way of running things (although not necessarily the best) when the core organization is small—under twenty people, perhaps—and closely gathered together so that personal communication is easy. Once things get much bigger than that, formality has to be increased, and the personal, telepathic, empathetic style is frustrated.

The key to success is having the right people, who blend with the core team and can act on their own. A lot of time is spent on selecting the right people and assessing whether they will fit in or not. It is no accident that some of the most successful club organizations have a nepotistic feel to them; they deliberately recruit people like themselves, even from the same family, so that the club remains a club.

> He came heralded by all—the charismatic spokesman for the oppressed people of the inner cities—to head up one of the big housing charities. An expert communicator, he was in demand everywhere and saw it as part of his job to raise the profile of the organization by his public appearances. So he traveled—and ran the organization on Fridays. With a series of brisk meetings, crisp memos, and tape-recorded messages to his secretary he raced through his week's in-box and was off again to spread the word or argue with governments.
>
> The world was impressed, but not the organization. Its members were not consulted. They hardly met this hero figure who was in their midst. They were dictated to, decided upon, budgeted for, without regard or say. They had been used to working in a collective, not a dictatorship. They rebelled.
>
> He was furious. They were stupid, inadequate, ungrateful. His teams in the past had understood him and his priorities. They had done things his way in his absence. Why not here? Let them go and he would find his own team, his own club. The organization came to blows. He went, not them, and it was everyone's loss.
>
> A spider needs a club—but it has to be its own club.

THE ROLE TRIBE

It is all very different in a role organization. Here the best picture is the kind of chart that all organizations have. It looks like a pyramid of boxes. Inside each box is a job title, with an individual's name in smaller type

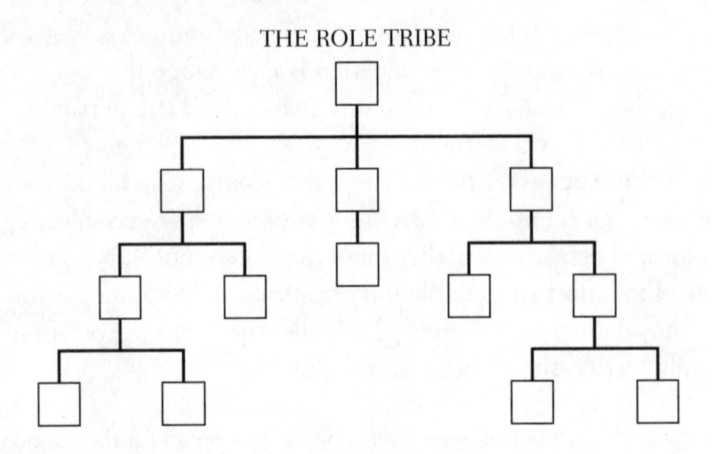
THE ROLE TRIBE

below, indicating who is currently the occupant of that box—but, of course, the box continues even if the individual departs.

The underlying organizational idea is that organizations are sets of roles or job-boxes, joined together in a logical and orderly fashion so that together they discharge the work of the organization. The organization is a piece of construction engineering, with role piled on role, and responsibility linked to responsibility. Individuals are "role occupants" with job descriptions that effectively lay down the requirements of the role and its boundaries. From time to time, as priorities change, the organization will rearrange the roles and their relationship to each other and then reallocate the individuals to the roles.

Communications in these cultures are formalized, as are systems and procedures. The memoranda go from role to role (head of X department to deputy head) and are copied to roles, not individuals. The place abounds in procedures for every eventuality, in rules and handbooks. There are standards, quality controls, and evaluation procedures. It is all managed rather than led.

Most mature organizations have a lot of the role tribe in them, because once an operation has settled down it can be routinized and, as it were, imprinted on the future. All organizations strive for predictability and certainty—for then fewer decisions are needed, everybody can get on with their job, the outcomes can be guaranteed and the inputs calculated.

You know where you are and where you will be; it is secure and comfortable, even if it is, at times, too predictable to be exciting.

These role organizations thrive when they are doing a routine, stable, and unchanging task, but they find it very hard to cope with change or with individual exceptions. If it's not in the rule book, they have to wait for the rule book to be rewritten before they can act. Administrative organizations, such as those making welfare payments or recording vehicle licenses, or those that keep the banking system running, record our electricity, or collect our taxes, have all got to be role organizations. They will prove very frustrating if you turn out to be one of those individual exceptions, but on the other hand, if the welfare system were administered by a host of club cultures, each responding as they saw fit, social justice would hardly be served. Efficiency and fairness in routine tasks demand a role culture.

The important thing in these cultures is to get the logic of the design right, the flow of work and procedures. People are, in one sense, a less critical factor. They can be trained to fit the role. Indeed, role organizations do not want too much independence or initiative. Railways want engineers whose trains arrive on time, not five minutes early. Role organizations want role occupants, not individualists.

THE TASK TRIBE

The task philosophy evolved in response to the need for an organizational form that could respond to change in a less individualistic way than a club tribe, and more speedily than a role organization.

The organizational idea is that a group, or team of talents and resources, should be applied to a project, problem, or task. In that way, each task gets the treatment it requires—it does not have to be standardized across the organization. The groups can also be changed, disbanded, or increased as the task changes. A net that can pull its cords this way and that, and regroup at will, is the picture of this tribe.

The task tribe is the preferred one for many competent people, because they work in groups, sharing both skills and responsibilities. They are constantly working on new challenges, since every task is different,

THE TASK TRIBE

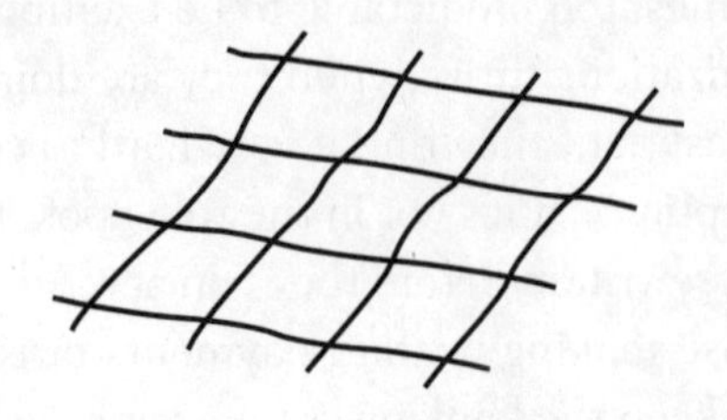

and thus keep themselves developing and enthusiastic. It is usually a warm and friendly place because it is built around cooperative groups of colleagues, without much overt hierarchy. There are plans rather than procedures, reviews of progress rather than assessments of past performance. It is a forward-looking philosophy for a developing organization.

The task philosophy thrives in situations where problem solving is the job of the organization. Consultancies, advertising agencies, construction firms, parts of journalism and the media, product development groups, surgical teams, in fact, any situation beyond the capacity of one person with minions to solve, which cannot be embodied in procedures, needs a task style.

The problem is that these tribes are expensive. They use professional, competent people who spend quite a lot of time talking together in search of the right solution. You would not use a task tribe to make a wheel, because the group would want to reinvent it, or at least improve on it, first. It is a questioning culture, which chafes at routines and the daily grind of administration or repetitive chores.

A task organization talks of coordinators and team leaders rather than managers; it is long on plans but short on job descriptions because the future is still uncertain. It wants commitment and rewards success with more assignments. It promises excitement and challenge but not security of employment, because it cannot afford to employ people who do not continually meet new challenges successfully. Task cultures, therefore, tend to be full of young, energetic people, developing and testing their talents: people who are self-confident enough not to worry about long-term security, at least not yet!

THE PERSON TRIBE

The person tribe is very different from the previous three. The other three put the organization's purpose first and then, in their different ways, harness the individual to this purpose. The person tribe philosophy puts the individual first and makes the organization the resource for the individual's talents. The most obvious examples are doctors who, for their own convenience, group themselves in a practice, lawyers or architects in partnerships, artists in a studio, and perhaps professors in a faculty, or scientists in a research laboratory.

Stars, loosely grouped in a cluster or constellation, are the image of a person organization.

The organizational idea behind it is that the individual talent is all-important but must be served by some sort of minimal organization. Person-style groups do not, in fact, like to use the word organization but find all sorts of alternative words: practice, partnership, faculty, and so on. Nor do they talk of managers but of secretaries, bursars, and chief clerks. Indeed, the managers of these organizations are always lower in status than the professionals. You may have a senior partner in a law office but if you ask for the manager you are likely to be shown into the chief clerk's office.

The individual professionals in these organizations usually have tenure—the legal right to keep their job until retirement. This means that the management is not only lower in status but has few, if any, formal means of control over the professionals. The professionals cannot be sacked and in many cases their salary is fixed by an outside body such as their professional association. In a university, for these reasons, the head of department or dean of faculty is usually a rotating job, often seen as a necessary chore rather than a mark of distinction.

In other words, a person organization is very difficult to run in any ordinary way. The professionals have to be held on a very light rein; they can be persuaded but not commanded, influenced, cajoled, or bargained with but not managed.

The style works where the talent of the individual is what matters, which is why you find it in the old professions, the arts, some sports, and some religions. Increasingly, however, some professions are finding that the problems the organization is asked to deal with are too complex for one individual's talents. To plan and construct a major inner-city shopping and entertainment complex is beyond the scope of one architect, however brilliant. Every construction site needs its quantity surveyors, its designers, its engineers, its insulation specialists, and many other experts, in addition to its architect. It is a time for teams, not individuals. Architects, specialized lawyers, and even the clergy group themselves into task organizations and submit themselves to more organized disciplines. It goes against their tribal instinct as stars but at least for them a task tribe is better than a role tribe. Remember, though, stars will remain stars at heart, reluctant to compromise their beliefs, individuals first and team members second, hard to manage but needed for their talents. As we get older many of us incline toward this sort of person tribe. A friend told me that he tried to build a consulting organization (usually a task tribe) using the skills and experience of retired executives.

"It was hopeless," he said, "they were happy to give their views or their technical advice, but always on a 'take it or leave it' basis. They would never compromise, never muck in with the team, never battle it through to get an agreed solution. Stars, yes. Team-makers, no."

THE MIX OF TRIBES

We will each have our favorite tribe of the four but we must always remember that no organization is tribally pure, nor should it be. The description of the tribes should help to explain why a person does not always fit neatly into the ways of an organization. Someone who has spent their formative years in a role organization will be incapacitated in the more intuitive, free-form atmosphere of a club organization, and vice versa.

SOME QUESTIONS FOR THINKING AND TALKING ABOUT

Getting organized requires that you have the right people in the right place.

1. Draw a symbolic picture of the organization you work in as it is now, giving the appropriate symbol to each part or division of the organization (for example, a club "web" at the top, with "nets" around it and a pyramid of boxes underneath). Compare your picture with those drawn by other people.
2. How would you like to change the picture to make the whole organization more effective? Do the others agree?
3. Which tribe best fits you? According to the theory outlined in this chapter, in which bits of the organization would you be most happy and most effective? How could you change your bit of the organization to make it fit you more closely?
4. Discuss your conclusions with your group. Do they agree?

" The first appraisal form that I filled in for someone working for me required me to score them from one to ten on eight different aspects of their work and then to discuss the scores with them. The last item on the list was loyalty. I gave him an eight.

'Why only an eight?' he asked me.

'Well, I don't think I ever noticed you being actively disloyal to the company but I don't believe that you are really prepared to commit your future to us, to give us that long-term loyalty.'

'Why should I?' he said. 'If that's the sort of total commitment you want then the company has to prove to me that it will repay my commitment to them with theirs to me. Actually,' he went on, 'I think that score ought to be the other way round. I ought to be scoring the company on the kind of loyalty it has earned from me. I think I would only give it a six.'

You cannot demand loyalty, I realized then, any more than you can command respect, or trust. They all have to be earned. **"**

16 Find Your God

I had the dubious privilege of a classical education. Not for me the experiments in the chemistry laboratory, the dissections of biology, or even the theorems of mathematics. I was steeped in Greek and Latin from the age of ten to twenty. Surely, I later reflected, there was *something* the Greeks knew that might be of use in organizations. There is. It is their religion.

The Greeks had many gods. Each person was free to follow the god of his or her own choice. There was, therefore, a god for metalworkers and another for musicians, a god for the lover of nature and another for lovers of wine. It was, you might say, a very liberal theology, but it had a point. You could choose your god, or goddess, to suit your talents and you would then probably find yourself with like-minded people, valuing similar things, celebrating in similar ways, obeying similar rules. Life has many aspects, as the Greeks saw it, and they had a god for each.

So it is in organizations. There is no one right way to manage. There are at least four ways, probably more. Each works well in its place, and less well out of its place. Each of us is more suited to one way than to the others, although we can do a bit of playacting when we have to. Put in the language of the Greeks, we each have our preferred god but we can worship other gods when we have to.

The four principal gods are Zeus, the king of the gods; Apollo, the god of harmony, but also of order and reason; Athena, the warrior goddess, patron of Ulysses; and Dionysus, the god who represents individual liberty and sometimes license. Followers of Zeus work better with each other than with followers of Apollo. If you want to be effective and comfortable, therefore, find your god, and then find his or her followers. There is a questionnaire at the end of this chapter that will help you to score yourself, and the part of the organization where you work, against each of the gods. This will show you whether you are, as one might put it, in the right temple or not.

This chapter is loosely connected with Chapter Fifteen, on tribes. Each god, as you will discover, fits best with one style of organization, with one picture. After reading these two chapters it should not be difficult to guess which god goes with which picture. The questionnaire, however, will spell it out.

ZEUS PEOPLE

Zeus people are personalities. Zeus himself was the king of the gods in ancient Greece; ruling by thunderbolt and showers of gold, he was a man of impulse and a lover of power. Zeus people are used to getting their own way by strength of personality, by promises or by force. A "jungle fighter" was the description Michael Maccoby, an American anthropologist, gave to this kind of character, when he started to look at organizations as tribes.

A Zeus is a personality and relies on personalities. He, or nowadays often she, will cultivate networks. He will have a bulging address book, will be endlessly on the telephone, will always be talking—to someone. Meetings will be short, small, and decisive, although it will be Zeus who decides. Zeus people will not write when they can talk; indeed many a Zeus is illiterate, preferring to *see* you listening and to be able to judge your reactions.

A Zeus relies on people to get things done, people he has power over or, more usually, people he can trust—his own gang. That way things get done and get done the way he wants them done. That way things happen fast, fewer controls are needed, fewer bits of paper, fewer bureaucratic meetings and permissions. The people, therefore, are vital and Zeus will spend a lot of time selecting the right people, people who are not only technically good but, even more important, people that he can work with and can trust.

Ron had for many years been a group trainer. His job had been to work with groups and individuals in organizations to develop their capacities and to improve their effectiveness. He was good at it.

After fifteen years, however, he needed a change. His aunt had died and left him some money. He invested it in a restaurant in a country town and became an owner/manager.

"Do you find that all your training skills are useful?" I asked him one day.

"Well, to tell you the truth," he said, "I find that it is much easier to get the right person to begin with than to get the wrong one and then train them to be better. So now I spend a lot of my time selecting the new people. I want people that I can rely on—I'm too busy to be checking and supervising them always."

"Quite a little Zeus, you've become," I said.

"What's that?"

"Oh, nothing," I replied, because I know that Zeus people do not like to think that there is a theory to explain what they are by instinct.

Zeus people at their best rely on trust. At their worst they are bullies, relying on power and the threat of power. A good Zeus is great to work with, and for, because they delegate hugely, control lightly, leave much to your discretion, reward results, and forgive genuine mistakes. Trust, however, is fragile. Break it and, like a cracked windowpane, it has to be replaced, not repaired. Zeus people know this instinctively and therefore have to get rid of those they can no longer rely on. "Hire and fire" it looks like, but it is essential to their style. Do not work for this character if you do not enjoy risks.

APOLLO PEOPLE

People of this type are quite different. Apollo was the god of harmony, of logic, of reason and, I'm afraid, of sheep. His followers like things to be tidy and ordered. Things should go by the book, everything that can be predicted should be planned for. Instinct is to be suspected because it is unpredictable and disrupts the nice order of things. Organizations, at their best, should be like railway timetables with all the trains running on time.

Apollo people are quite content to be known by job title because that describes their position in the scheme of things. They like organization charts, manuals, and job descriptions because that keeps things in their place. To an Apollonian, routine is desirable and efficient. Whenever a routine can be introduced, sensibly, it should be.

Apollo people are most comfortable in those parts of organizations where stability and predictability are assumed and encouraged. The accounting department, the factory and the warehouse, the bank till and the back office tend to be full of Apollonians. A Zeus would chafe and then upset the system by ignoring a rule or failing to enter a figure in a column.

We should thank God for Apollonians. It is they who are content to do many of the essential jobs in organizations, to be the interchangeable human parts that we need to keep the wheels moving. In return they value the security that goes with predictable jobs, the feeling that they can catch the same bus home every evening, that they can take their holiday as usual during the first two weeks of August, that their pension scheme is safe and is waiting for them. They enjoy committees and can be relied upon to check the small print of contracts and of minutes, because they value accuracy and order. Don't work with them if you are untidy, impulsive, or impatient, but never despise them.

I once worked with a lot of Apollonians. Everyone left the office on the dot of 5:20 P.M. I had a three-page job description telling me all the things I had to look after but ending with the phrase "authority to spend up to $50 on his own initiative" which made it clear that, while I had many things to process, I could not do anything about them on my own. I was one of those indispensable cogs. It was safe, secure, but boring.

So I went job hunting.

"Why not come and join us?" a friend said. "We are looking for an economist."

"Who is 'us'?" I asked.

"An investment bank," he replied, "specializing in the developing countries."

"But I'm not an economist. I studied Greek and Latin at university."

"Ah, but it was Oxford, wasn't it?" he said, as if that made it all right. "Come and have lunch with us all on Tuesday."

I went. We talked about many things but not the job. We got on quite well. Next week they offered me the job as "development economist." It was a new post. Two months later I joined them.

They gave me a nice office, a secretary, and the *Financial Times*—and then left me alone. Nobody phoned, there were no memos, no letters, nothing. After a week I went to see my friend.

"It's very nice to be here—" I began.

"Good to have you," he replied.

"But . . ."

"Well?"

"I wonder if I could see my job description, get an idea of my reporting relationships, my responsibilities, the general organization structure."

"What on earth are you talking about?" he replied, looking surprised. "We don't use all that jargon here—what's worrying you?"

"Well, what am I supposed to be doing?" I blurted out, in desperation.

"Why, what the rest of us do," he said. "Search out new opportunities, get out and meet people, sniff out the possible allies, find out where the action is in these countries—bring some of it to us. OK?"

"OK," I said. But it wasn't. I was still an Apollonian shoved in among a gang of Zeus worshippers. I was in the wrong temple, and I soon left.

ATHENA PEOPLE

Athena people are different again. Athena was the patron goddess of Ulysses, the intrepid adventurer. She is the warrior goddess, favored by task forces and commando units, standing for camaraderie in battle, for problem solving, for teams and project groups, for adventure and new horizons.

Athena people are excited by what is new. They like new problems and new situations. But they are also team people. They know that complex problems need a mix of talents to solve them, a task force. In this task force they will pick all the talents they may need and then seek to weld them into a team. Teams are fun. If the team wins, all win. If it fails, all fail. There is a sense of solidarity, and of equality, since each person has a contribution to make.

Athenians are not interested in your length of service or your title, they only want to know what you are good at and whether you are committed to the task in hand. Youth, energy, and creativity are often the hallmark of an Athenian team, the sort of people you might find in a consultancy, in an advertising agency or a merchant bank.

Athenians love novelty. They are quickly bored by routine or by repetitive tasks that offer no challenge to their problem-solving skills. They want the space to experiment and the freedom to work in their own way. Achievement is their goal, rather than power or promotion. Their security comes not from their contracts of employment, as with Apollonians, nor from their relationship to any Zeus, but from their own competence. They know that they are only as good as their last assignment, so it had better be well done.

As a result, Athenians work hard and long. Work is often their play. Do not marry one unless you are in their team as well because you will never see them otherwise. Even their leisure has to be turned into a sequence of team challenges—Athenians find it hard to be in a room alone.

Athenians are not slaves. They want to solve problems, not carry out other people's solutions. Each task has to be of their own creation if they are to give it their commitment. They are, therefore, expensive and uncooperative cogs, and should not be used as such.

> A group of young interior designers was asked, as part of their training, to erect and decorate a temporary theater that had been designed by an architect for a local drama group. It was a simple task because all the materials were precisely specified and the plan was meticulous in its detail. All that could have been foreseen was foreseen.
>
> The designers shuddered. The thought of erecting someone else's design was very unpleasant. They found every fault they could with it. In the end, they redesigned it from scratch. Only then were they prepared to start erecting it. As a result it was finished two weeks late and ran well over its budget. They had infuriated the architect, frustrated the drama group, and let down their own instructors.

DIONYSUS PEOPLE

Most interesting of all are Dionysus people. Dionysus (Bacchus to the Romans) was the god of wine and of festivals, often at midnight on the mountainside. For me, however, he is the god of the individual, of the free spirit. Dionysians do not like organizations. They will tolerate them only if the organization is necessary for them to do their work. Architects, lawyers, doctors, professors will, if they have to, work in organizations, but they see the organization as serving them rather than the other way round. Conversely, they are tolerated by organizations only because their talents and expertise are essential.

To a Dionysian, the quality of the work is paramount. One cannot compromise, they feel, with the truth. They are craftsmen, obsessed with their craft, uninterested in power or position as long as they have enough to guarantee them their freedom to work as they wish. In their organizations (partnerships, universities, bits of the civil service), *manager* is a low-status word applied only to the service functions (catering manager, transport manager) with words like *partner* or *principal* or even *secretary* signifying seniority. This is because Dionysians recognize colleagues, even senior colleagues, but not a "boss." They are not to be managed in any conventional way. They are team players when they have to be but, like all craftsmen, they prefer to be allowed to get on with their work in their own way; the loners in the organization's cast list, looking for respect and influence and freedom.

Organizations find Dionysians uncomfortable. They do not respond to the traditional carrots and sticks of promotions and reprimands. They seem to have a loyalty to their craft or profession that overrides their commitment to the organization. They are only tolerated because they are good; they are the artists of the organizational world.

> Have families changed their character? There was a time when the head of the family was expected to be a Zeus. People were expected to do as he wanted, when he wanted, and it was always "he," seldom "she." Carrots and sticks, or thunderbolts and showers of gold, were his weapons.
>
> Then Apollo became the fashion. To each his duties and status. The man made the money, the woman made the food, the children made the beds.
>
> Democracy bred Athenians. Not duties now, but common tasks and projects, joint decisions—"Why don't we . . . ?" And now is Dionysus the fashion? Are we all individuals now, none more equal than others, eating when we want, making our own music in our own place, the home a collection of individual interests, just a base for everyone's enthusiasms?

SOME QUESTIONS FOR THINKING AND TALKING ABOUT

Getting organized requires that you know the sort of characters you and the people who surround you are. Use this questionnaire to help you find out who your gods are.

Consider the organization you work for, the whole of it. Look at the four statements under each of the following nine headings in the questionnaire. Rank the four statements in order of "best fit" to the organization as you see it (that is, put "1" against the statement that best fits your organization, "2" against the next best, and so on). Put the figures in the column headed "Organization."

When you have done this for the organization, then go through the whole process again, this time for yourself, reflecting your *own* preferences and beliefs. Put the figures in the column headed "Self." Try not to look at your rankings under "Organization" as you do this, so your second ranking is truly independent.*

When you have ranked all the statements under each of the two columns add up the scores for all the statements that are marked (a) under each heading, then the scores for all the statements listed as (b), and so on (for example, a total score of 9 for all the (b) statements would mean that you had ranked the (b) statement "1" in each of the nine headings).

You should now be able to complete the following table.

	(a) statements	**(b) statements**	**(c) statements**	**(d) statements**	**Totals**
Organization					**90**
Self					**90**

As in most questionnaires, you will want to qualify many of your answers with the remark, "it all depends. . . ." You will find it hard, in some instances, to find any great difference in your own mind between some of the statements. Don't let this deter you. The questionnaire results will not be precisely accurate, but they should provide useful indications. You will find that the best way to proceed when trying to rank each set of statements is to trust your first, almost intuitive reactions. Don't linger over them too long.

When you have completed the questionnaire and added up the totals, turn to page 139 for an explanation of the scores.

*The questionnaire is based on one originally developed by Dr. Roger Harrison.

1. A good boss	**Organization**	**Self**
(a) is strong, decisive, and firm but fair. He or she is protective, generous, and indulgent to loyal subordinates.	________	________
(b) is impersonal and correct, avoiding the exercise of authority for personal advantage. He or she demands from subordinates only that which is required by the formal system.	________	________
(c) is open to influence in matters concerning the task. He or she uses personal authority to obtain the resources needed to get on with the job.	________	________
(d) is concerned and responsive to the personal needs and values of others. He or she sees it as part of the job to provide satisfying and growth-stimulating work opportunities for subordinates.	________	________

2. A good subordinate		
(a) is hard-working, loyal to the interests of the superior, resourceful, and trustworthy.	________	________
(b) is responsible and reliable, meeting the duties and responsibilities of his or her job and avoiding actions that surprise or embarrass the superior.	________	________
(c) is self-motivated to contribute his or her best to the task and is open with ideas and suggestions. He or she is		

	Organization	Self
nevertheless willing to let others lead when they show greater expertise or ability.	______	______
(d) is vitally interested in the development of his or her own potential and is open to learning and receiving help. He or she also respects the needs and values of others and is willing to give help and contribute to their development as well.	______	______

3. A good member of the organization gives first priority to

	Organization	Self
(a) the personal demands of the boss.	______	______
(b) the duties, responsibilities, and requirements of the employee's own role, and the customary standards of personal behavior.	______	______
(c) the task of the group, team, or project.	______	______
(d) the personal needs of the individuals involved.	______	______

4. People who do well in the organization

	Organization	Self
(a) are politically aware, and like taking risks and operating on their own.	______	______
(b) are conscientious and responsible, with a strong sense of loyalty to the organization.	______	______
(c) are technically competent and effective, with a strong commitment to getting the job done.	______	______

	Organization	Self
(d) are effective and competent in personal relationships, with a strong commitment to the growth and development of individual talents.	______	______
5. The organization treats the individual		
(a) as a trusted agent whose time and energy are at the disposal of those who run the organization.	______	______
(b) as though his or her time and energy were available through a contract, having rights and responsibilities on both sides.	______	______
(c) as a coworker who has committed his or her skills and abilities to the common cause.	______	______
(d) as an interesting and talented person in his or her own right.	______	______
6. People are controlled and influenced by		
(a) the personal exercise of rewards, reprimands, or charisma.	______	______
(b) the impersonal exercise of economic and political power to enforce procedures and standards of performance.	______	______
(c) communication and discussion of task requirements leading to appropriate action motivated by personal commitment to goal achievement.	______	______

	Organization	Self
(d) intrinsic interest and enjoyment in the activities to be done, concern and caring for the needs of the other people involved, or both.	______	______

7. It is legitimate for one person to control another's activities

(a) if he or she has more power and influence in the organization.	______	______
(b) if his or her role prescribes responsibility for directing the other.	______	______
(c) if he or she has more knowledge relevant to the task at hand.	______	______
(d) if he or she is accepted by those he or she controls.	______	______

8. The basis of task assignment is

(a) the personal needs and judgment of those who run the place.	______	______
(b) the formal divisions of functions and responsibility in the system.	______	______
(c) the resource and expertise requirements of the job to be done.	______	______
(d) the personal wishes and needs for learning and growth of the individual organization members.	______	______

9. Competition

(a) is for personal power and advantage.	______	______
(b) is for high-status position in the formal system.	______	______

	Organization	**Self**
(c) is for excellence of contribution to the task.	________	________
(d) is for attention to one's own personal needs.	________	________

Now interpret the questionnaire scores: the (a) statements represent Zeus and the club tribe; the (b) statements represent Apollo and the role tribe; the (c) statements represent Athena and the task tribe; and the (d) statements represent Dionysus and the person tribe. The lower the total scores for any set of statements, the more prevalent that god is in your organization, or in you. A score of 9 for the (a) statements (the lowest possible total) would mean a totally pure Zeus world. You are unlikely to have any totals as low as that.

A table might look like this:

	(a) statements	**(b) statements**	**(c) statements**	**(d) statements**	**Total**
Organization	16	12	27	35	**90**
Self	29	24	16	21	**90**

This table would mean that your organization was a mix of Apollonians and Zeus people, while you prefer to follow Athena backed up by Dionysus.

“My son has a very different pattern to his day than I do. He likes to get up very late in the morning and go to bed very late at night. It is not that he sleeps more, he points out, just that he does it at different hours. He works better that way, he says, it is his biorhythms that are different.

‘It’s highly inconvenient,’ I say. ‘It means that I can’t discuss things with you before lunch, that no one can. Half the world has stopped work before you’ve really got going. I don’t know how you’ll ever fit into an organization.’

‘Is it better,’ he asks, ‘for me to be at my best, or to be below par but at your convenience?’ It is a good question.

‘Your best will need to be very good indeed,’ I reply, in the end, ‘if I, and others, are to put up with the inconvenience.’

‘It will be,’ he says, confidently. I don’t know whether to be pleased or worried.

How tolerant of someone’s idiosyncrasies can one expect an organization to be?”

17 Counting and Costing

"What did that cost?" I asked suspiciously as she removed a piece of furniture from the back of the car. Auction days in the local town were always a bit dangerous.

"It's not a cost at all," she said. "It's an investment."

"Hmm," I said, "investments usually produce some income—I can't see this one doing that."

"No, but it will double in value, you'll see. You should be grateful."

"Calling something an investment doesn't make the check any smaller."

"No, but it feels much better," she smiled at me.

"If we have any more investments like this," I retorted, "we'll be so rich in assets that we won't have any cash to buy the food."

My nephew had started studying economics at school. He had expected it to be boring but at the end of term he said to me, "How do people get on in the world if they've never heard of opportunity cost?" He had experienced one of those glimpses of the obvious that make sense of the world around. Sadly, I told him, a lot of people have not had the glimpse—they struggle on, they muddle through, but they miss out on a lot of possibilities.

A cost is what you make it, but what you decide to make it can make all the difference. Accountancy turns out to be more of an art than a science. It is, I often think, a great pity that accountants have made their art more mysterious than it really is because more ordinary mortals are then tempted to think it is beyond their grasp. It is not, and it must not be seen as such a mystery—the way you decide to count or cost something can be vital, whether you are a business or a family or anything in between. "Count the cost," we say, but seldom go on to add that there are many different ways to do it. We can choose which way we count every cost.

INVESTMENT OR EXPENDITURE?

The cash paid out is the same, but if we call it an investment then we are asserting that we are increasing the value of our assets in some way. We have not then lost our money, merely converted it into another sort of currency. It is as if we had invested it in a savings account, even if the savings account equivalent is actually a piece of furniture, a car, or a new shed. It is for this reason that accountants show investments as part of the assets in the balance sheet, not as expenses in the income statement.

Some assets go up in value, like antiques; some go down, like a new car. The amount that they depreciate in value each year is therefore really a cost because you are losing that bit of the money you originally spent. Depreciation, therefore, is a cost in the accounts even though no cash goes out—one of the many paradoxes of accounting. It is important to remember that your car is costing you money through depreciation even though you may not be using it at all. If no notice is taken of this invisible cost you will think your driving is costing you less than it really is.

It is not always immediately obvious whether something is an investment or a cost. A new lawnmower for the college grounds no doubt does add to the college assets, but what would it be worth if it had to be sold in a year's time? It might be more realistic to call it a cost, like the gasoline you put into it, something that you need but once the money is spent you won't see it again.

Should people be a cost or an investment? Every organization treats them as a cost, yet in some cases they are very obvious assets. Football clubs sell their players to other clubs for big sums of money. Film stars are insured by the movie companies, as are key personnel in major businesses. Clearly they are assets. Do such assets grow in value or do they depreciate?

Down the ages people have been costs, and costs are something that one tries to reduce. If we really saw people as assets, as an investment, it might make a huge difference to the way we treat them because investments are something to be constantly improved, cared for, and have money spent on. Companies are now buying other companies for their *intellectual property*—their ideas, their inventions, and their creations. In the end intellectual property means people. Soon, I am sure, some businesses will be putting their people on their balance sheet, not their cost statement. It could make all the difference.

VARIABLE OR FIXED?

Every time I use the telephone it costs me money—so much per minute depending on the time of day and the distance of the call. That is the variable cost of the telephone. However, even if I never use it at all, I still pay a monthly charge to the telephone company for the line into my house. That is the fixed cost.

It looks simple, but it is not always obvious whether a cost is variable or fixed and it can make a difference, a big difference. I have to travel into town most days. I have a choice. I can buy a ticket each day, in which case my travel is a variable cost, or I can buy a season ticket good for the whole year, in which case it is a fixed cost that is the same no matter how many journeys I make. I have calculated that since I do not travel every day, the cost of a season ticket works out at a little more per journey than the ordinary ticket. Nevertheless I still bought the season ticket. Why? I knew that once I had bought the season ticket the variable cost of each journey would be zero. I would not therefore have to make big decisions about whether any particular journey was worth it or not; the extra ones would, in a sense, be free. As a result, I now probably travel far too much!

In general, treating something as a fixed cost reduces the variable cost to zero. If, therefore, a foreign company decides that, come what may, it is going to have a major sales force and twenty offices in this country for at least ten years, then that is a fixed cost allocated over x million sales. Any extra sales cost almost nothing to sell. Therefore it can cut the price on those extra sales and still make money. Competitors will complain of price-cutting and dumping, and will say that they do not see how anyone can make money at that price. The company can do it only because it has arbitrarily decided to call the major expenditure a fixed cost.

ABOVE COST OR BELOW PRICE?

One main reason for counting your costs is to know what price you should charge for your product or your service. At first glance it is obvious that one should price it a little above the cost. But that is not as easy as it seems. As we have seen, one can arrive at a situation where all the fixed costs have been recovered, the variable costs are very low for extra sales, and so a very low price can be fixed. Marginal cost pricing, this is called. Tempting but dangerous.

> Sandra had trained as an interior designer and was now in business on her own, working from her own home. She charged a small fee for advice and took her profit from a commission on materials and labor provided. Her costs were low. A room and a car she already had, plus a computer and a telephone and all the paraphernalia of a modern little office. In fact, anything she made was, as she put it, "gravy." As a result she felt able to cut her prices to her customers, which she felt was only fair because she was still inexperienced, and anyway she wanted the business.
>
> The gravy money was nice. It even paid for a holiday for her and her husband in Greece. Sitting by the harbor, she said she now felt confident enough to rent a proper office, hire an assistant, and run a proper business.
>
> "I can afford it," she said.

> "Let's see the sums," he said. "But you're working for nothing," he said after a bit. "There's nothing here for your salary. It's more work for the same amount of gravy. That doesn't make sense."
>
> "It's true," reflected Sandra, "my prices create good gravy but no meat. I've locked myself into a trap."

It gets more complicated. Every business, whatever its size, can choose to set its prices above its proper costs (whatever those are), or at or below the prices of its competitors. Monopolies, naturally, price above their maximum costs. There lies the danger, for if the costs are not monitored externally there is every temptation to let them grow inexorably. All businesses naturally seek to create mini-monopolies by developing products or services that are unique. A full cure for AIDS could, today, command its own price because it would be in great demand and would have no competitors. So might a special brand of mustard, if it were seen to be special enough to be unique.

More often, however, one is forced to fix one's price by the competition. This is the so-called discipline of the marketplace. The challenge then is to get one's costs below the price that has to be set. The danger here is that we subconsciously fiddle the costs. How does this happen, one may ask, if we are honest with ourselves and accurate in our counting? Quite easily. The fixed costs come in blocks, salaries, rent, heating, and so on. They have to be split over all the sales to arrive at a unit cost. It is always tempting to overestimate sales, thereby reducing unit cost. It can lead to quick bankruptcy.

No one should sell anything until they have calculated their break-even point. This is the point that sales at a certain price have to reach to cover both their variable costs and all the fixed costs. Profit only starts when the break-even point is reached. Too many businesses never get to it—either they were too optimistic or they did not know it was there.

REAL COSTS OR OPPORTUNITY COSTS?

It is relatively easy to know what you are spending or are going to spend. It is less easy to calculate what you are losing by spending in this way—the lost opportunity. The opportunity cost of a long holiday is sometimes a missed business venture or a vital invitation to dinner, which is perhaps why ambitious people seldom take long holidays.

Opportunity costs are invisible costs. They do not appear in any accounts. They are hard to calculate. Most obviously they arise when a business can make only one of three possible investments—the others are lost opportunities. More fundamentally, every time we say yes to one course of action we are saying no to other possibilities. Our lives are full of opportunities not seized. We would do well, in life as well as business, to think, "What am I missing if I do this?" It is important, however, not to get mesmerized by the question or we would end up doing nothing.

> Trevor was sixteen. He wanted to leave school. Lessons and exams were not his thing.
>
> "I've seen this advertisement," he said. "The supermarkets want young people. They'll pay them well, treat them well, train them. It's real money. I could leave home."
>
> "Don't do it," his headmaster said. "You'll regret it later on. You'll need more than a bit of training in a supermarket if you want to really make a success of your life. Don't sell the rest of your life for some money now."
>
> "The future will take care of itself. This is my opportunity."
>
> "Yes, but the opportunity has a cost. Unfortunately, you won't know the cost until it's too late."

PROFIT OR CASH?

"Are profit and cash not the same?" I asked. "Unfortunately, no, so you must count them both." It was that realization that saved me from at least one disaster.

Every business, indeed every organization and every family, needs to make a profit eventually. The money coming in must, in the end, be more than the money going out or we starve. It is that little phrase "in the end" that makes all the difference. It is, for instance, quite possible to make a theoretical profit in one year and still spend much more money than you earn, if a lot of that money is spent on investments, or new assets. Profit, after all, is only the measurement of income and costs, but investments, as we have seen, are not costs.

Businesses can easily be profitable but have no money. They then have to borrow money, the cost of which makes them unprofitable. It is essential, therefore, to keep an eye on the cash, and particularly the cash *flow.* Cash is the blood of any organization. If it ceases to flow the organization dies. On the other hand, if you only watch the cash, you take a very short-term view because some cash, when it is turned into investments, takes a long time to come back to you.

Government treasuries are strangely obsessed with cash and cash flow. The money coming in must balance the money going out. There is little heed given to arguments that the expenditure of money now might result in less money being needed in five years' time. Cash flow is what concerns them, not the relative profitability of investments over the longer term. As a result, policy is inevitably short term in many areas.

Families who think only in cash flow terms and the weekly paycheck also find it hard to justify long-term investments, in housing, for instance, or in training. In the short term it is always more cash-efficient to rent than to buy, but in the long term it is a bad investment, unprofitable, money down the drain.

Money and its manipulations will always be something of a mystery. Much of it is best left to professionals. Not the essentials, however. No one should be in charge of money and its spending who does not understand the basic choices that have to be made. In the end these are not mysterious at all—just common sense.

SOME QUESTIONS FOR THINKING AND TALKING ABOUT

Getting organized requires that one be clear about the different options in matters concerning money, its earning and its spending.

1. Look at your own personal expenditure over the last year.
   a. Which of it was investment, which of it straight expenditure?
   b. Would you like to have changed the balance?
2. Examine the costs for one product, service, or activity in your organization.

a. Which are the fixed and which the variable costs?
b. Would you want to change any of them around?
c. If you did, what difference would it make?

3. Draw up a cash-flow chart for the next year in your own life. For each month there should be a set of inflows and outflows. Can you identify the good times and the bad times to come? Can you do anything to change the times of the cash flows to get a better balance?

"We were students, impoverished students, in Boston, Massachusetts. To help our finances my wife went into partnership with a friend in Britain to print and market the brass rubbings from some old English churches.

The friend in Britain made rubbings of the brasses and then, by a silk-screen process, printed them onto four-foot sheets of parchment paper. Fitted with rods at top and bottom these could be hung as scrolls or they could be put into large picture frames. She sent a hundred to Boston as a first batch.

My wife was responsible for the marketing. The first decision was the price. We knew all the costs. They came to $1.90 each, landed in Boston. I suggested we sell them for $2.50, which allowed for a 30 percent margin (more than adequate, in my view). She took the problem to the marketing class in the Business School. They used it as a class problem, did some market research, and recommended a price of $40. Anything less, they said, would make it look cheap in the eyes of the customer.

Instead of selling a thousand at 60 cents profit (total profit $600) we sold a hundred at over $38 profit (total profit $3,810) and had much more fun.

Pricing, I realized, is as much psychology as it is accounting."

18 The Customer Is Always There

"Let's make no mistake about it, this charity is a business." It was the chairman talking, addressing the senior officers of the foundation. They were silent, slightly shocked, I think. Then one of them spoke.

"But we don't make a profit. We aren't meant to make a profit."

"The real purpose of any business," he replied, "is not to make profits but to provide the goods and services that its customers need and want. The profits that it makes allow it to stay in business, they are truthfully only a means to an end. With the profits the business can buy equipment, invest in research, pay dividends to its financiers, and reward its workforce. Profit is the new money for the enterprise. This enterprise," he went on, "is only different in that its new money comes from donations—from old friends and new well-wishers. I have to tell you, however, that if we were not efficient in carrying out our job we wouldn't get that new money—just like any other business." They went away thoughtful. So did I.

In the world that I grew up in, customers were people who queued in shops, hoping that there would still be some left when their turn came. Businessmen were glorified car salesmen, pouring scorn on your trade-in and praising their own product, all in order to make as much money as possible out of the deal. I grew up disliking both customers and businessmen and hoping to be neither. In the end, of course, I am both. We all are. It need not be bad news.

I now know that nothing in life has any purpose if it is not done, ultimately, for someone else. We may make what we think is a most ingenious chair, but if no one wants to sit on it, let alone buy it, it will inevitably end up in some rubbish heap. Lives that touch no one else are lonely lives, sad lives, empty lives. In that big sense we all need customers.

I now know, too, that customers are hard to come by and that, once lost, they seldom return. Of course, if I have something no one else has then they will line up to get it and I can be as offensive as I like, as extortionate as I like, a ticket scalper at Wimbledon, perhaps. But all monopolies are temporary. There will be other ticket scalpers if not other Wimbledons. The railway has a monopoly until someone builds a road, and then an airport. I have no wish to be a temporary scalper of tickets.

It was Deming and Juran, two American consultants, who convinced the Japanese thirty years ago that in the long term satisfied customers were good for business because they, or their friends, would come back for more. Think of what you would like if you were them, they said, give them quality, give them reliability, give them promises you can keep. It may be more expensive to start with, but you will still be there when others are not because your customers will need you. It worked.

CUSTOMERS ARE FOREVER

This was my first lesson—we must treat our clients or our customers as if they were going to be there forever. Any faults would show up in the end so there must be no faults. I used to think it acceptable if 90 percent of the output was OK, until someone asked me if I would fly on an airline which boasted of a 90 percent safety record. We take it for granted that airlines aim for 100 percent safety and are shocked if they fail, but accept that the Postal Service is reasonable in aiming to get 90 percent of first class mail to its destination within the next three days. "Zero defects," says Crosby, an expert on quality, "have to be the standard for every operation."

If customers are forever we would be wise to listen to what they have to say.

> John, a friend, had one particularly difficult customer when he first started his picture framing business. He kept coming back to point out how it could have been done better and to demand that John do it again. He would bring examples of other work and ask why John could not do it as well or better but cheaper.
>
> "It's that awful Mr. Woolcroft again," he complained to his wife one evening. "He is impossible. I have spent so much time and trouble on his pictures that I might as well have given them to him for all the profit I make out of them."
>
> "Poor you," she said, "but your frames are getting much better with all his prodding and complaining."
>
> "Oh, yes—I'm certainly learning something from the jerk."
>
> "Perhaps, then, you ought to be paying him?" she said, mischievously.
>
> "Oh, shut up and go to sleep!"

Some retailers are very demanding customers to their many suppliers. They determine what standards they want, they provide advice and send along their own inspectors to see how the work is done.

"Is that not a great imposition?" I asked one German textile manufacturer.

"Not at all," he replied. "We appreciate it enormously, it helps us improve standards and that helps the rest of our business."

Good products, whatever they are, make good clients—and good clients keep you in business, whatever you are doing.

CUSTOMERS ARE EVERYWHERE

This was the second lesson. Customers are not only the people in the supermarket or the salesroom, people who answer ads, or who buy package holidays. Every parent is a customer of the school their children go to, every patient is a customer of the doctor or the hospital, every reader is a customer of the writer, every unemployed person is a customer of the job center, and every commuter is a customer of the rail or bus service. It does not always feel like that.

> Come to the hospital at 2:20 P.M., they said. The time seemed precise, so I was punctual. So, it appeared, were twenty others, all given the same time, all asked to sit in a bare waiting room until their names were called. After one hour I went to ask when I might be seen.
>
> "Another eight names before yours," she said.
>
> "Then why did you ask me to get here at two twenty when it seems that no one is going to get round to me until four o'clock?"
>
> "We can't keep the doctors waiting," she replied. "Their time is precious."
>
> "And what about my time?" I asked.
>
> "Your time?" she repeated, looking blank. "I don't understand."
>
> I gave up, sat, and waited.

For too many institutions the recipient of their services is still a nuisance. "You should have seen this hospital before they let the patients in—it was spotless." Or they see themselves as monopolies, privileged monopolies, access to which is a favor, something to be grateful for. Organizations thinking like that, however, miss a trick or two. We all need feedback, some response to our work, preferably a good response. Without it work is a chore and a bore, something to be got rid of, not enjoyed. There is nothing quite so satisfying as the response of a gratified customer—or client, parent, student, job-seeker, or handicapped, homeless, sick, or poor person whom you are trying to do something for.

> One business arranges for the people who make the machine tool in the factory to deliver it in person to the customer. Their trip disrupts the work in the factory, but the effect on the workforce's morale of meeting the people who will use their product more than compensates for this. And the fact that they are going to make quite sure that they do not arrive with a dud machine, plus the further fact that they are the best people to make sure that the customer installs it correctly, does wonders for customer relations.

Customers are everywhere, not just on the outside. When I started work in a large business it took me some time to realize that most of my customers were in fact inside the organization—other colleagues, other departments. If I took their requirements and their wishes seriously I would be of much more use to them and the organization, I would be doing my own job properly. It was a revelation. I was at the time in the training department. I had seen my job as being the administration of a number of programs, which included making sure that each department sent a representative on each program—something that required quite a lot of reminding, prodding, and nagging. These people were not, to me, my customers but the storehouses of the raw material for my courses—storehouses with very stiff doors! With my new insight I set up a series of meetings in which I asked them to help me design more effective programs and to arrange for me to have pre-program meetings with the immediate customers—the prospective trainees. All blockages ceased, I was overbooked. The feedback from the courses improved, their status went up, I got promoted.

We can in fact look at our jobs, whether in the office, the shop, or the home, as being surrounded by customers or clients, each of them expecting something of us, often in return for something else. Do we take them seriously as customers? Do we try to find out what would best suit their needs? Do we try to adapt our ways to suit their wants? Do we actively look for some feedback or evaluation of what we do? Do we discuss the implied contract with them—if I do this, will you do that in return?

It may sound peculiar for the accountant to see the line manager as a customer and not an enemy, but the change in perspective can bring about a big change in behavior. I cook, in the holidays, because I enjoy it. I enjoy it partly because I cook for my friends and my family—they are my customers. I want to bring them satisfaction and happiness. It works—their satisfaction feeds my contentment. Cooking remains a pleasure when it would be easy for it to become a chore.

CUSTOMERS COME FIRST

I used to think that if you designed a better mousetrap the world would beat a path to your door. The product came first, then you sold it, if you had to. I remember the consternation in the university when it was suggested that they should appoint a marketing officer. "That would be a public sign of failure," said a professor. "The world would know that we could not fill our courses."

Wise businesses today shape their product to the customers they want. They look for their *market niche,* a particular product for a particular type of client or customer. That policy requires them to find ways of talking and listening to their potential customers, allowing them to influence their thinking. Wise schools, wise hospitals, wise charities do the same. If they find the right customers and listen to them, their product sells itself. In the jargon of a business, good marketing makes selling easy.

Not all organizations are wise. Not many years ago I found a notice on the gate of a primary school. "No parents beyond this point," it said. "Why not?" I asked. "Because they don't want to get involved and we don't want them involved, it only complicates things." Not surprisingly, they were complaining of falling enrollments. Few schools adopt that policy today, but there are still hospitals that treat patients as products, not as customers, there are welfare officers who see their queues as a nuisance, not as clients wanting service, there are shops where "take it or leave it" seems to be the dominant attitude. The views of the customer are not wanted in these organizations—they are inconvenient.

> "I wish the airlines would not keep calling me a customer," said Wendy. "I'm a passenger. And I'm a patient at the doctor's, not his customer, and I'm a parent at my son's school, not their stupid customer."

"What's wrong with being a customer?"

"It sounds as if they are only after my money," she said. "Everyone has gone money-mad."

"You're wrong," I said, "they use the word customer because they want to emphasize that they are now trying to give you proper value for your money, to put your interests first, to take you seriously, not as a piece of freight or a statistic in the waiting room."

"You could have fooled me," she said.

Words are tricky things. It is wiser to get the actions right before we change the language, rather than the other way round.

Experts find it particularly difficult to see why nonexperts should have any influence over what they do. Museums, in most places, continue to be laid out in a way that suits the experts. If a new director reorganizes the displays to make them more accessible to a nonexpert public he or she can be accused of "popularizing" and "demeaning" the standards of the museum. What happens in museums happens almost everywhere. This is the way it should be, says the expert, I will not compromise my standards.

Sometimes the experts are right. The production department should never compromise on safety or quality standards to allow the sales manager (*their* customer) to quote a lower price. Sometimes the experts accept that their way will be appreciated by only a tiny few, a minuscule market niche, but they prefer it that way. The argument then should not be about which way is better but about which type of customer we want. The customer decision is the first decision, not the last.

The grand plans and corporate strategies of companies have to start with decisions about customers. How many do we want; what do they want and what will they be prepared to pay? Where are they? How different are they one from the other, how many differences can we tolerate? Ultimately, every customer may be able to have a tailor-made product. Cars roll off the mass production lines today, each one different, each one "customized" to give every purchaser a choice of specification, of extras, and of color. With well over a hundred television channels available via satellite, every individual can have their own viewing pattern and every program will increasingly be made with a very precise audience in mind. It will be no use making the best documentary if no one is going to pay to watch it. More and more the customer is coming first.

> I used to write books to show my colleagues and competitors how clever I was. They did not sell, nor were my colleagues very impressed. Today I write with a very particular audience in mind. My colleagues are still rude—"academic turned popular journalist," they say. I reply with the old quip, "My sins may be scarlet but my books just might be read." What I have done has been to change, quite deliberately, my choice of customer. If I had wanted academic prestige I might have continued to write for the five or six experts who would have been interested. I decided otherwise. The choice of customer is always the first choice.

SOME QUESTIONS FOR THINKING AND TALKING ABOUT

Getting organized requires that you be clear about who the customers are, both for you and for the organization.

1. List the different kinds of customers or clients of your organization. Could there be others? Who?
2. How seriously does the organization treat these customers? Give examples (research, feedback, visits). Could it do more? If so, what?
3. Think about your internal clients:
   a. Who are they?
   b. Do you know what they expect of you?
   c. Are you giving it to them?
   d. How could you treat them more seriously as clients?

“‘If you have to get a job you will disappoint me,’ I told my young daughter the other day. She looked at me, startled.

‘But I thought you did not approve of people being deliberately unemployed,’ she said, ‘welfare layabouts, I heard you call them.’

‘I didn’t say anything about not working. I want you to look for *customers,* not jobs. If you can make something or do something that other people are prepared to pay good money for, you will be greatly encouraged; your security will then be in your own keeping, not in the hands of others. And ironically,’ I went on, ‘if you find that you can get customers, then lots of people will want to employ you, jobs will come easy if it is jobs that you want. You may find, of course, that when you’ve got customers, jobs are boring.’

‘I’m not sure that my skills are saleable,’ she said ruefully.

‘Oh, yes, they are. You’ve been thinking jobs and qualifications. Try thinking customers instead and you’ll be surprised how many things you can think of to offer them.’”

19 Curiosity Made the Cat

"When I became a man," wrote St. Paul to the Corinthians nearly two thousand years ago, "I put away childish things"—like learning, I thought, when I first heard those words, and all that belonged to schools: clothes that you did not want to wear, or food that you would never order if you had any choice, or cold rooms and bullies. "Never again," I sang, as I walked out of the school gates for the last time. No more would I have to memorize dates and facts and numbers, no more guessing at the answer the teacher had in the back of the book, no more formulas or tables or drills. Learning was done with. I was a man.

I was wrong, of course. I was doubly wrong, in fact. Learning had only just begun, but it was not the sort of learning I had been used to. At school I knew one thing for sure, that every problem in the world had already been solved by someone. The answers to many of them were in the teacher's head or in the back of their textbook. If they were not, then they were bound to be in someone else's head or in someone else's book. The message I carried away with me was clear—if you meet with an unfamiliar problem, find the expert, usually someone older or senior to yourself, and ask them.

It was a crippling message. Until I unlearned it—at about the age of thirty-five—I was a meek underling, obedient on the whole but dull, unaware of my own capabilities and sometimes doubting whether I had any. I had "learned," or thought I had, that people in higher jobs than me inevitably knew more than me and inevitably were right. I had acquired for myself the *assumption of stupidity*—my stupidity—when what I really needed was the *habit of curiosity*.

We all assume that we know how we learn. It could be said that a *theory of learning* sits, unspoken and unrealized, deep in all of us. Unfortunately, it is often the wrong theory. I have just given some clues to one wrong theory; you could call it the *sponge theory*—soak up all the knowledge and skills that are poured over you and then squeeze yourself to reproduce them, losing a bit in the process. "Now learn this," my old master would say, writing something on the blackboard. We were expected to write it down, memorize it, and then, one day, reproduce it, 40 percent being OK for a pass.

I now know, and it was one of those shafts of understanding that change your life, that learning is not like that at all. It is much more like a wheel that is kept in motion by a series of jolts. As the wheel moves, so we learn and so we grow; the faster it moves, the faster we grow. That all sounds rather obvious but the lessons behind it turn out to be crucial to our own development and to keeping any organization effective.

The wheel of learning looks like this:

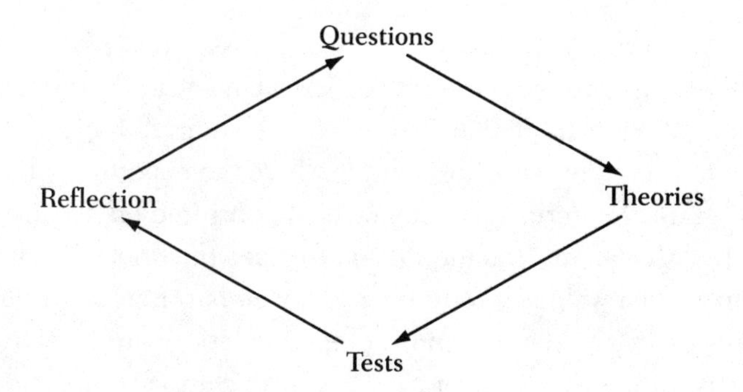

QUESTIONS

The wheel of learning starts with questions that are jolted into being by curiosity, or the need to know. Those who ask no questions get told no lies—maybe—but they also add nothing to their understanding of the world. Children abound in curiosity and as a result it is said that half of all we ever learn is learned by the time we are seven. Is that because we lose the habit of curiosity as we grow older or is it somehow drummed out of us?

THEORIES

Questions need answers, or at least possible answers or theories. These need not be grand scientific formulations but merely "because" statements; "water boils because it reaches 212°F" is a perfectly acceptable working theory. (It could provoke another question, "*Why* does it boil at 212°F," but it could do very well on its own to serve the purposes of the discussion.) Theories are fed by knowledge and jolted along by ideas. Uninformed theories are a waste of time, or worse, can do damage because they are plain wrong. The theories stage of the wheel of learning is used as the justification for my classroom experience but, sadly, theories that are not answers to questions are all too forgettable; they have no hook to hang on and so fall to the ground.

TESTS

Theories need tests to see if they really work. Untested, they remain interesting ideas, dreams in fact; and "dreams give wings to fools" as my children used to keep reminding me. This is where the opportunity to practice is so important. I can read all the books ever printed on bricklaying but until I actually try to mix the mortar and to place the bricks I will not have learned to build a wall, as I found out to my embarrassment. Book learning is derided by the realists and the pragmatists of life as being only a partial substitute for the real thing. They are right to see it is only a part, but wrong to dismiss it as unnecessary because tests without any well-formed ideas or theories are just random experimentation. You may be able to find out how to drive a car by just getting into it and pushing some knobs and pedals, but I would prefer not to be a pedestrian in the vicinity!

REFLECTION

Reflection, the last stage of the wheel, is essential if the learning is to be cemented into one's understanding. It can be an unconscious or an automatic process, done so spontaneously that we would not want to dignify it with the term "reflection." If the shot goes wide of the target to the left it is an automatic reaction to adjust one's aim to the right and then to test it again. Everything we do is really a test of some assumption. If it does not work we should ask why, modify our assumptions, and try again. We don't because we get lazy. That way, however, we do not learn.

Put like this, the process of learning—questions, theories, tests, and reflections—looks rather obvious and unexciting. People, however, can easily get stuck in one or other bit of the wheel, or take shortcuts across it.

> Daniel was the organization's "sniffer." He could find a problem everywhere, or if not a problem at least a hint of a suspicion and certainly a question. You could bet your shirt on Daniel questioning one of the statements in a presentation and on his being the first to say, "Why could we not . . . ?" No one could say that his questions were irrelevant, but since he never saw it as his job to provide any of the answers, his interjections were usually greeted by a groan and, in time, were disregarded. Daniel was one of nature's "quizzers"—but never got the credit for it, because he was stuck at that part of the wheel.

> Auriol was the department's resident expert. No one who knew the place would be silly enough to prepare a customer proposal without checking with Auriol. It was not just that she had a file index where most people had a memory, she also had the ability to put some of her file cards together and come up with a completely new idea or new way of approaching the problem. "Talk to Auriol," the newcomer was told, "but don't ask her what to do, she hates decisions." To select one idea meant,

for Auriol, discarding the others, so she seldom tested her theories, leaving that to others. Nor was she a great instigator, having few questions herself she preferred to respond to others; a born academic, they said, and did not promote her. She, too, was stuck on the wheel.

"You're just a journalist," my academic friend sneered when I stated that my interest was in seeing whether any of my ideas were actually used by people who worked in organizations, whether the ideas answered any of the questions that mattered to them. To an academic, a journalist is a trivializer, more interested in impact than in truth, a slur on the academic's profession. To a journalist, however, in another proud profession, to be called an academic is equally insulting, implying that one is out of touch with reality, pursuing knowledge for its own sake, irrespective of its relevance or interest to others. It all depends on which part of the wheel interests you.

Unfortunately there are *brakes* to this wheel, brakes that in some organizations and in some families seem to be permanently on. One of them is the *they syndrome,* the feeling that someone else is responsible for solving the problem or even for taking care of one's destiny.

Mary was divorcing her husband, who was a private in the army.

Where would she live, I asked, when she had to leave her army married quarters.

"They haven't told me yet," she replied.

"Who is this 'they'?" I asked.

"They haven't told me yet, who 'they' is, have they?" she replied scornfully, irritated that I could be so stupid.

I laughed, but then I, too, had reacted like that long ago. I was waiting outside the personnel department in my oil company when an old friend passed by.

"What are you waiting for?" he said.

"To see what they have in store for me," I replied.

"Take my advice," he said. "Don't rely on 'them,' whoever 'they' are, take charge of your own future."

I did, and I started to learn, to ask questions, to look for ideas and the opportunities to test them—to move the wheel.

It is easy to put a brake on curiosity. Call it impertinent or frivolous or time-wasting, because other people's questions are seldom comfortable to those in power. The same goes for new ideas, unless they are one's own. Organizations that insist on doing things by the book (*their* ideas), that look for obedience and discipline without question, and that provide people with little discretion for testing out any new ways or new thoughts are effectively stopping the wheel of learning in its tracks.

My first job in Malaysia was not a real job. I was instructed to visit all the company's depots and offices and get to know how things worked and some of the people who worked in them, and then report back. I was determined to make a good impression and I was delighted to stumble upon a gap in the distribution logic, or so it seemed to me. I worked out my sums and, sure enough, there was a much more efficient way of distributing paraffin in bulk by rail, instead of in cans by car. All it needed was a small amount of investment in new facilities. I presented my report and my proposal to the operations manager in Singapore. He hardly glanced at it.

"How long have you been out here, Handy?" he asked.

"Six months, sir," I replied.

"And how long has this company been operating here?"

"Fifty years, I think, sir."

"Fifty-two, to be precise. And do you really think that in your six months you have been able to find a better way than we have after fifty-two years?"

"Er, I suppose not, sir. Sorry, sir."

The interview ended. My curiosity had been killed along with any interest in new ideas or in opportunities to test them. Afterward I remember investing a lot more time in my social life but even then I knew that my learning had stopped. The wheel had ground to a halt.

Learning needs *forgiveness* to keep the wheel turning. I asked the American chief executive of a particularly dynamic bank to tell me the secret of his people policy. Forgiveness, he said, looking me straight in the eyes, a great hunk of a man. I looked startled. "Sure," he said. "We have to give these guys a lot of discretion because there is not time to keep tabs on all they do. We expect them to ask questions, to come up with new ideas, to take risks and to make their own judgments. Sometimes they get it wrong, inevitably. That's when we forgive them, as long as we feel they have learned something. Mind you," he went on, "there was one person who managed to lend half of our net worth to Brazil. We didn't forgive him!" Too many organizations neither forgive nor forget, unaware that by so doing they are putting brakes on the wheel, because learning needs space, the room to test and the freedom to get it wrong.

Learning also needs a *proper selfishness.* By this I do not mean that you should put yourself first at any cost, but rather have a sense of responsibility for yourself and enough self-confidence to believe that you *can* get what you want in life.

There is good evidence that the people who learn best are those who

a. Take responsibility for themselves and for their future.
b. Have a clear view of what they want that future to be.
c. Want to make sure that they get it.
d. Believe that they can.

They do not leave it to some unseen "they," they push the wheel around themselves.

Learning, I have gradually discovered, is not what I had thought it was at school. Learning is *not* just knowing the answers (Mastermind learning). It is *not* the same as training or studying, which can just mean learning the answers to other people's questions. It is bigger than both.

Learning does *not* happen automatically, through living. It requires energy, thought, courage, self-confidence, and support. It is easy to give up on it, and so cease to grow.

Learning is *not* measured by examinations, which test only the theories stage, but by experience as it is tested and understood.

Learning is *not* finding out what other people already know, but is the process of solving our own problems. It occurs by questioning, searching, testing, and reflecting until the answers become part of us. That is how we grow and become all that we are capable of being.

Organizations that encourage the wheel of learning, that relish curiosity, questions, and ideas, that allow space for experiment and for reflection, that forgive mistakes and promote self-confidence, these are the learning organizations, and theirs is a competitive advantage no one can steal from them.

Individuals who have enough will and enough confidence to push the wheel are the individuals who get most out of life, even if it is at times uncomfortable and unpopular because they are taking charge of their own destinies. It was only when I began to understand this that my life began to blossom. Would that it had happened sooner.

SOME QUESTIONS FOR THINKING AND TALKING ABOUT

Getting organized requires that one make the most of oneself and of everyone else, that learning be truly encouraged and promoted.

1. Try to recall one instance when the wheel of learning turned full circle for you, starting with a question and ending with reflection on the outcomes. Now recall another instance where the sequence got blocked.
   a. Can you identify the reasons for the blockage?
   b. Can you point out the circumstances that produced the successful instance?
2. Looking at your own organization, or even your own family, are there any brakes that need releasing?
   a. Who is not learning as well as they might? Why not?
   b. What could be done to encourage more curiosity, more ideas, more practice, and more feedback, the four jolts to the wheel?
3. Ask the same questions of other members of the group. How do their answers compare with yours? What actions could you take as a group, independently of the organization?
4. Think about your own learning patterns:
   a. What do *you,* individually, now need to do more of or less of?
   b. What would help you to change?
   c. Whom should you speak to?

“My first job posting was to Kuala Lumpur, the capital of Malaysia. The head office then employed some 150 people and controlled a further five branch offices. I was the newest raw recruit, straight from the home office, knowing nothing.

Ian was the general manager, aged thirty-five—unconventional and earmarked, so they said, for the very top. He had asked to see me first thing.

‘For your first month here,’ he said, after greeting me very warmly, ‘I want you to sit in this room, in that corner there, and to be as inconspicuous as possible. Don’t speak when anyone else is in the room, and never, on any account, leave the room, no matter what is going on. You will learn more about this business from watching me for a month than by sitting by some other Nelly, and I will learn too from having to explain to you what is going on and why I did what I did. Feel free, when we are alone, to ask me any questions that are on your mind. And one thing—keep a diary with your impressions, lessons learned, resolutions made. That will serve as your report on the month—except that I don’t want to see it, it will be your report to yourself.’

It was a fascinating month. I watched a union negotiation, the sacking of a sales manager for dishonesty, the planning of a new refinery—and many other smaller things. I also learned, could not fail to learn, some important lessons in management, the biggest of which was the thrill of being trusted.

Some day, I said to myself in my report, I will trust some young person as Ian has trusted me.”

20 Shamrocks Galore

It was thirty years ago, in a great oil company. I was being given an overseas assignment. I had a busy day ahead, appointments with the doctor, the company doctor, that was, on the eighteenth floor, then a visit to the travel department on the second floor to collect my visa and my tickets, which they would have ready for me, a quick stop with the income tax (personal) section on the third floor to sign a few forms for the Internal Revenue Service and Social Security, which our tax people had prepared for me, and, last, a session with the housing section who would be sending their people down next week to inspect my modest flat before putting it on the rental market for me.

It seemed natural, in those days. Big companies employed all their own services. If you wanted to control something, you owned it. It made life much easier, for everyone. Everything could be done in-house, by employees of the same company, bonded together by the same loyalties like one big army. Indeed, in those days, that oil company employed, worldwide, twice as many people as the whole British Army.

It also made it expensive. The oil company paid well, and its conditions of service applied just as much to the clerks in the travel department as to the geologists exploring for oil in the jungle.

It was also likely to be inefficient. These internal service businesses were small monopolies. They never needed to compare their costs with outside businesses. They had no prices, but were just one part of the general overhead of being in business. It was fine for the company as long as those costs could be recovered from the prices of the products.

> It was my first proper assignment in the head office of the South-East Asian region of the company. I was to fix the prices for all the lubricating oils the company sold in that part of the world. It seemed a most important task. I soon discovered that it was simplicity itself. I was given a sheet with all the cost items that went into the price—one list for each type of oil. I then obtained the actual numbers for each item from the accounts department, added them up and filled in the last item on the sheet, which was "Profit Margin: 15%." Add this onto the cost total and you had your prices.
>
> "But surely," I said to the sales manager, "that means that the more we spend on our cost, the higher our profit?"
>
> "Of course," he said, "but never put it like that—we are only recovering our costs and taking a small percentage. It sounds better."
>
> It was my first experience of a monopoly.

Competition came to that industry eventually, when supply began to outstrip demand throughout the world. Nowadays companies get preferential terms from their chosen travel agents, but they don't own those travel agents. My successors would be expected to visit their own doctor, consult their own tax expert, fill in their own forms. No longer are such things part of the general cost of being in business, not unless you are still a monopoly.

Companies have increasingly taken on a shamrock shape. Shamrocks are the Irish clover, the Irish national emblem, originally used by St. Patrick to demonstrate that just as the three leaves were still part of one leaf, so the three aspects of God were still the same God. Today it is a symbolic way of saying that there are three very different types of workforce involved in any business, but that they still need to be seen as one combined workforce.

The shamrock's three leaves represent

- The core workforce
- The contractual fringe
- The flexible labor force

Each is vital, each is different, each is part of a larger whole. A major strategic problem for a business today is to decide what functions, and what people, belong in each. And what is happening to business, because of the competitive pressures, is also happening to more and more organizations outside business as they too are exposed to economic realities.

THE CORE WORKFORCE

This is made up of those people—managers, technicians, and skilled workers—who are essential to the company. They give the organization its uniqueness. Because they are essential the organization seeks to bind them to itself, with good pay, good perks, good conditions. In return it asks for flexibility—go here, do this, muck in—on the workfloor just as much as in the executive offices. It asks also for commitment and hard work. The core workforce are the people who do not see their home in daylight for half of the year, whose children remember them as the person who comes to lunch on Sundays, who wonder what has happened to the leisure society they keep reading about.

Because they are expensive, however, there are fewer of them. Every successful business has quadrupled its turnover in the last ten years yet halved its core workforce—putting even greater strains on those left in. It is not a cozy life in the core these days, even if there is some guarantee of employment.

THE CONTRACTUAL FRINGE

This part of the shamrock has picked up more and more of the work. There is, after all, no sense in giving the high rates of pay and the privileged conditions of the core to people doing tasks that can be equally well done from outside the organization.

It starts with the drivers and the cleaners. There are specialist organizations that will do these things as well as one can do them oneself, or better—and usually cheaper. But it can go much further. Most manufacturing firms are now really design and assembly organizations with a wide range of suppliers, and it is but a small step from suppliers of "things" to suppliers of "activities." Toyota, in Japan, has thirty thousand subcontractors, having, in the new jargon, *outsourced* most of its work.

It can go too far. One German manufacturer of garden equipment subcontracted not only the bits of the tools he sold but also the assembly. He franchised the sales operation, giving people the agency for a particular region; he employed a professional firm to do the accounting and a design consultancy to do the design work. He was left with his Mercedes and a car telephone, having done away with the office. Going to these extremes can be dangerous because you might lose control, but it shows you what can be done.

What to contract out and what to keep in the core, as one's uniqueness, is not an easy decision. Many companies contract out their strategic plans—to consultants. Are they wise thus to let go of their future or do they need the outside expertise? It will be a different answer for different people, but it is hard to justify keeping specialist people or groups in the core who are only needed occasionally—better to set them up as independent operations and buy back the time you need from them. And because they are off the pension plan and off the premises it is actually possible to pay such people much more per day or per week than they were earning as employees and still save money. It is therefore one of those rare cases in business when no one loses under the new arrangements.

THE FLEXIBLE LABOR FORCE

This is the third leaf of the shamrock. Again, it makes no economic sense to have your core workers doing extra to cover the peak periods of activity, nor to store up enough workers to be able to cope with any peak without overtime. Core workers will be expensive and their overtime very expensive. Cheaper by far, although less convenient to the manager and supervisor, to hire in occasional help, part-time or temporary, at lower rates.

That has the sound of exploitation about it, of getting labor cheap. It can be, but it is not always resented by the labor. Many people like part-time work, provided that they don't have to rely on it for all of their support. Women with children at school, people with books to write or crafts to do who need to bring in some form of income while they do it, pensioners who rejoice in three days' work a week and would not want any more, the person who wants eight months' hard labor in the winter and four months to spend the money in the summer. In other words, people who want to keep flexibility in their lives by putting together two or more bits of part-time work.

The flexible labor force is growing. It currently amounts to something like one-quarter of all paid workers in some industrialized countries. If you add to the flexible labor force all the self-employed, who are mostly in the contractual fringe of organizations, you will find that over one-third of paid workers in these countries are not actually in conventional full-time jobs. The way things are going it may well be that there will be more people working *outside* the core than *inside* it. The shamrock is beginning to make itself felt, everywhere.

> Schools could, and perhaps should, become shamrocks. One reason for making schools larger, and therefore difficult to manage, is the need to provide a wide range of options for the students. A range of fifteen subjects spread over six years ends up by requiring twelve hundred students in the whole school to justify all the teachers required. That is a big organization. Schools do not, however, have to employ all those teachers. They could contract out a lot of specialist instruction, keeping for themselves the core subjects and the care and control of the students. Languages, for instance, may well be best taught in special language centers, word processing in secretarial colleges, physical education in gymnasiums—none need to be in the traditional school system. Schools could use their money not to hire more teachers, but to buy slots at outside learning agencies of all sorts. That way they could adjust their spending to fit the changing requirements of their student population instead of trying to fit their students' needs to the staff they happen to have available.

Organizations have to realize that each leaf of the shamrock is different and needs to be handled differently. The contractual fringe is controlled by a careful monitoring of *outputs.* The organization needs to be sure that the things or the activities it has ordered are of the right quality, are on time and are charged at the price agreed. How the subcontractor achieves these results is not the concern of the organization, unless it affects the end result.

Control the results, not the process—the "what," not the "how." The message is simple and obvious. Most managers, however, accustomed only to managing people and things in the core, have been used to controlling the "how" in order to get the right "what"—in the belief that if you have the right process and procedures you will get the right result. Letting go of the "how" seems, to them, to be letting go control. It is not, it is just a different way of managing—the way purchasing offices have always managed, come to that. Sadly, and mistakenly, the purchasing manager has seldom been highly regarded in business, nor highly paid, nor even highly trained. Shamrock organizations have to be purchasing organizations, purchasing things and activities. It is a different way of managing.

The flexible labor force, in its turn, needs a different type of management. Without permanent constraints, with no possibility of promotion and no security, they cannot be expected to give the organization the kind of commitment and loyalty one would hope to find in the core. They are—have to be—the hired help. It is important to begin with, that the rates are good, that they are treated as individuals with control over their lives and not as temporary slave labor. That is not enough, however. If they are going to respect the traditions and standards of the organization they have to know what these are, they cannot be expected to pick them up or to search them out. They are, after all, only there for the beer.

> A big retail chain had found the solution to staffing its stores. It had a tiny core staff of managers and supervisors and a changing battalion of part-timers and temps. That way no one got bored—they weren't around long enough—and the managers could adjust their staffing requirements to the season, the day of the week, and even to the weather. There was an abundant labor market, particularly among the young who liked the flexible pattern and did not want to be tied to one particular job or firm.

> The managers went too far, however. The customers started to complain. The new staff did not know all the procedures, they knew and cared little about what they were selling, they were unhelpful and uncooperative and seemed to have no understanding of the tradition of service the chain had been at pains to establish over the years. Part-timers and temps, they realized, can only help out, they cannot replace the core staff.

The core staff members are increasingly precious. There are fewer of them. Each is, therefore, responsible for more. They are less easily replaced because they carry with them a chunk of the organization's memory. They are no longer interchangeable human parts, to be slotted in as and when necessary. In a real sense, they *are* the organization, even if it is legally owned and financed by outsiders. They need, therefore, to be treated as partners, if not by law then certainly by custom and by practice. Without their agreement and involvement things will not happen.

The core of the shamrock will therefore increasingly resemble professional organizations—those places where talented and qualified people are the real assets, the intellectual property of the organization. Such organizations are flat—most have only four layers or levels, from junior, to qualified, to senior, to partner. They work in teams, shifting teams, teams where even a partner can be a junior member if his or her contribution is not essential. They respect individuals, encouraging them to have their own clients, to sign their own work, to be their own people, not just cogs in the wheel. One should think of television teams, who hire in a lot of specialist help, but whose central core is made up of talented individuals working *with* rather than *for* other people.

Shamrocks are less convenient to manage than the old-fashioned organization. No longer are all the people you need all around you. No longer can you call a meeting for one hour's time and expect that they will all be there. Because the core is busier and more individual, because so many key people are now in the contractual fringe, meeting dates have to be negotiated or planned well in advance. No longer, in the shamrock, can one use overtime to cover up for inefficiencies or bad planning—the flexible labor force also has to be planned in advance and is always a very visible, and separate, item of cost. Shamrocks, therefore, are welcomed by few managers—they find them inconvenient. Trade unions see them as cutting employment, individuals fear that they will be displaced. Customers like to think that everything is there in one place. Economics, however, is a hard taskmaster, and once the shamrock is in place it is unlikely to be disinvented. Like it or not, it is the new way to get organized.

SOME QUESTIONS FOR THINKING AND TALKING ABOUT

Getting organized requires that one think along shamrock lines, whether one is a giant corporation or a solitary individual. A little analysis helps.

1. Think about the tasks in your area of responsibility:
   a. Which tasks could be done by outsiders—outsiders that may be other organizations or may be individuals?
   b. How would you measure such work? How would you put a price on it?
   c. List the options for each task.
2. Is any overtime worked in your area of responsibility? Could any of it be handled by part-timers or temporary workers? What would be the advantages? What would be the difficulties?
3. If you yourself were to move into the contractual fringe, what would you sell (things or skills or activities) and to whom? What would be the difficulties for you?

“As chairman of a health authority, Stephen had a problem. There was not enough money to pay for all the consultants they needed in their hospitals and too much of it was going to the oldest but not always, or any longer, the best. Too many potential consultants were fed up with waiting their turn. Morale was dangerously low.

Why not, suggested Stephen, be radical and pay all consultants only the basic salary, no increments, no merit awards, no bonuses? We will pay all these extras, he said, in time, not in money. Thus the old and distinguished would only have to work three days for their salary, the young and ambitious would work six. That way we could have twice as many consultants, with the old giving their wisdom and the young their energy. Those paid in time could use it to do private work or to play golf. It could be their time to use their way.

They laughed at him. But it's happening everywhere, I told him. I know senior people who are put on half-time at their same basic salary.

'We need you, Jim,' they told one of my friends, 'we need your experience, your contacts, your wisdom, but we only need it on Tuesdays, Jim; only Tuesdays.'

In wisdom roles you don't need to be full-time to be fully useful. Time, at some stages in life, can be more valuable than money.”

21 Portfolios and Flexi-Lives

"What do you do?" I asked her.

"I write plays for television," she said, "and I'm working on a novel." I looked at her admiringly—these were things I had once aspired to do until the shortage of talent and money persuaded me otherwise. She must have seen my look of admiration because she added, quickly, "Not that I've persuaded anyone to buy them yet, or even to look at them."

"What do you do for money, then?" I asked.

"Oh, I pack eggs on Sundays," she said. "It's awfully boring but it pays rather well."

When I asked her what she did, she told me first of her enthusiasm, not her source of income. I was startled. She was young, starting to make her way in life. At her age I had been desperate to find a secure source of income and unconvinced that anyone would be rash enough to offer me one. Enthusiasms had to take second place.

I remember cabling my parents (one still sent cables in those times) to announce my selection as a trainee oil executive. They were startled. "But I thought you wanted to write," my mother said. "That will have to come later," I replied. It did. Much later. For the next chunk of life I was going to be an oil executive, my income source defined me and described me, publicly at least. I would never have said, "I'm a writer, but I earn my money as an oilman."

Life is different, for me and for many others, today. I can and do now say, "I am a writer, but I earn most of my money doing other things." I am a portfolio person, I say, meaning that my work portfolio has different types of work within it, just as a share portfolio has a range of shares; some for income, some for security, some with risk attached for capital growth, or like an artist's portfolio with different specimens of different types of work that the artist can do.

Bits and pieces of work make up my portfolio: some obsess me, like my writing; some are there because I care, work done for free for societies or communities or charities; some are there because they bring in money and I would not do them if they didn't; some are genuine enthusiasms, like cooking or gardening—both forms of work that others charge money for; some are chores or obligations, like maintaining the house or doing routine administration. My portfolio and my life are balanced when there is enough money coming in, and when what I enjoy doing is proportionately a much bigger part of the portfolio than the chores and the duties.

That has always been true, of course, of me and of everyone else—the difference now is that I can change the balance if I want or need to. Before, when I joined my oil company, I bought *their* portfolio, like it or lump it, because they bought the greater part of my working and indeed waking time.

"Bits and pieces of work, that's not much of a career," said a friend. No, it isn't, not if a career means a progression up a ladder of jobs. But it is a great career if career means a succession of interesting projects over the years—some satisfied customers there, a new idea successfully pioneered that year, the house redone one year, the garden redesigned another, the children launched into school, a small business started, an overseas adventure, a training course completed, a new business partnership investigated—the list of projects ranges from strict business to purely domestic but it all adds up to a life, a career too rich to be summarized by the kind of résumé you might send to a new employer.

Work, looked at this way, is not simply work done for money. Work is effort and energy that is deliberately applied. Is playing football work, then? Certainly it is for the professional, whose income depends on it, but it is also work for the serious player who trains hard for it and who cares if he wins or loses. The fact that he does it from choice and not necessity only makes it good work, not menial work. We are not playing with words here. The redefinition of work in modern society is changing the way we look at our lives and at our priorities. It is important, therefore, that individuals, organizations, and governments understand what is going on. This redefinition is not happening because some dictionary compiler or some grammarian thought it would be a good idea, but because people themselves are beginning to use the word in a different way.

> "I've got so much work to do," said my uncle, one year into his retirement, "that I don't know how I ever had time to work."
>
> I looked at him, puzzled. "What do you mean, you've got so much work that you can't find time for work?"
>
> He laughed. "Yes, it does sound silly when you put it like that. I suppose that I'm really talking about different sorts of work. I've got so many things that I want to do and now have time to do, that I could not fit in going to that wretched office even if I had to."

Work used to mean things that we *had* to do, or were paid to do, usually for other people. Now it increasingly also means things that we *choose* to do. That little shift makes all the difference. For one thing, it means that no one need ever be out of work. They may be out of money, but that is less demoralizing than having nothing to do, and, actually, easier to do something about. The link between money and work is being stretched and, in many cases, broken. It is, for instance, socially acceptable—even respectable—for older people to collect money, their pension rights, for doing no paid work but to be very busy, like my uncle, doing work for free.

Why does this matter? It matters because more and more work is going to be done in bits and pieces. More and more people will therefore have to get their income and their satisfaction from putting together collections of these bits and pieces. People will find themselves jolted into flexi-lives: lives where each month, or even week, is different, with a different mix of bits and pieces; lives where there will be no fixed routine, no daily commuter train or bus to catch as regular as clockwork; lives where there will be frantic deadlines to meet one week and spare time galore the next; lives where a diary is a necessity to keep track of where you are meant to be, and where a telephone is essential. Some people, of course, have always lived like this.

> "I don't see what's so new about your so-called flexi-life," she said. "I've always lived one, had to. Look," she pointed to the big calendar hanging up in the kitchen, with a square for every day. Two or three things were written, scribbled really, in each square, in different colored inks.
>
> "Why the colors?" I asked.
>
> "Oh, that's my private system. Red is for the kids' things—school, outings, their friends coming to tea. Green is my stuff, my course at the local college and the three mornings I work in the shop. Then there's blue for social life and going out—precious little of that, you'll notice—and brown for all the boring things like the plumber and the bill for the insurance."
>
> "It's a sort of wall datebook," I said.
>
> "Sure—I might have made a fortune if I'd patented it—I just never realized it was anything new."

Organizations of all sorts are reducing the numbers of their permanent staff (see Chapter Twenty). They are discovering that they do not need all the people around all the time to get the work done. Some are needed only occasionally, for advice and consultation. Some are needed only at peak times or in odd and unsocial hours to help out. Others do not need to come into the office every day, or into the school or hospital or factory, to do their work, but can do it elsewhere in their own time and bring it in on certain days.

Some people like it that way. Mothers of small children prefer flexiwork, the ability to work where and when they can, to bring the work home rather than to go into the office to do it, to choose to work when the children are in bed, not in the daytime, to go out when there is someone else at home, not when the office demands it. If organizations want the skills and talents of such people, as they increasingly will, then they will move more and more toward devising bits and pieces of work for them.

Some people are having it thrust upon them. Many careers are now ending for people in their fifties. They are simply becoming too expensive to have around all the time when they also have to be given somewhere to sit, kept warm, provided with coffee, with secretarial help maybe, given a pension and often a car. Thrust, against their will, outside the organization, they find that most organizations are only prepared to offer them bits and pieces of work. Portfolio careers are forced upon them, not from choice but from necessity. Some, though not all, come to like it.

Some people have never known it any other way. Journalists, actors, artists, musicians, television camera crews, some architects and builders, plumbers, painters, carpenters, craftspeople of all sorts, indeed any self-employed person in any trade or profession, knows only too well that their business is a portfolio of bits and pieces of work, some big and long-lasting, some small and irregular. They have known no other way and would usually hate to trade their freedom, despite its uncertainty, for the security of full-time employment with a boss and a contract.

It seems likely that most people working today will become portfolio people for some part of their working lives, like it or not. The earlier they put a toe into the water, with a bit of self-employment on the edges, the easier they will find the transition.

It also seems inevitable that organizations will continue to share out more work in bits and pieces. They need to think more carefully about how to shape those bits and pieces, how to measure and price them. They also need to think about some of the implications, the effects on their buildings, for instance.

Offices are people's daytime homes, whether they be called a bank or a sales organization, a school or a town hall. Some are rather nice daytime homes with private apartments for all and better tea and coffee than one gets in one's real home. Some are more like boarding schools with large dormitories and with fodder rather than food. Either way, they were built on the assumption that they would be fully occupied. They never have been fully occupied for all the time. If most of the people were there for forty hours a week the organization was doing well. That is crazy economics at the best of times. No one would build a hotel that was only going to be used for 40 out of 168 hours every week. It gets more crazy when one-third to one-half of the people are out and about, doing their business, not sitting in their rooms. All that expensive space—empty!

> "My office is not an apartment building," said Marianne, head of a design business, "that is too expensive. Mine is more like a clubhouse. There are lots of rooms anyone can use, places to talk or eat or use our expensive computers, but every few private rooms. It is public space for members, the employees. They come in when they need to, for meetings or ideas or to use the services, but a lot of the time they are out and about with clients or experts, or are working at home. This way, I need a smaller building, I can furnish it better and, by the way, there is wonderful food—that brings them in if nothing else does." A club, not an office. It sounds nice too.

Marianne's employees, however, will take time to get used to it. They will miss their private bits of territory at the new clubhouse and will have to provide this for themselves at home. Marianne's challenge is to make the new shared territory better than the old tiny boxes that passed as offices.

Portfolios of work—the idea allowed me to make sense of my life, to put together my different interests in a pattern that had some meaning and predictability. I now see more and more people having to get their portfolios together. If they thought of them in that way, I believe they would find it easier and more satisfactory.

Managers, in their turn, need to realize that there are alternatives to employing one more person, burdening the overheads. People can be offered bits and pieces of work, can do a job for three days a week, bring work in rather than come in to do it, can telecommute, not rail-commute. It is, inevitably, more complicated to manage a batch of portfolio people than a corridor of wage-slaves, but it is cheaper, often more stimulating, and definitely the way things are going.

SOME QUESTIONS FOR THINKING AND TALKING ABOUT

Getting organized can mean rethinking the way you organize your work and that of other people.

1. What is your own current work portfolio? Include every kind of work. Would you like to change the balance? How?
2. Do any of your acquaintances lead an independent portfolio life? List the items in their portfolios. What are the problems?
3. As a manager could you break up some jobs into bits and pieces, suitable for someone's portfolio? Use one job as an example.
   a. How would you define the bits?
   b. Where, when, and how would they be done?
   c. How would you pay?

"'It is very good of you,' I said, 'to give this charity so much of your time, and particularly of your working time.' I was speaking to the CEO of a big commercial concern who sat on our council on the second Monday of every month.

'Oh, it's good for me—gets me out of the office—broadens my outlook. Besides, we believe that we have an obligation to put something back into the community.'

Indeed. But what I did not tell him, then, was that the local school, at my urging, had asked his company to let a couple of their young engineers spend a half-day twice a month working on a project and had been turned down flat. None of their people, he said, could spare the time.

Why, I wondered, was what was good for the managing director not good for the engineers? We all need to get out of the office. We all need to broaden our outlook. We all need to put something back into the community. Should these be privileges reserved for those who have made it?"

Epilogue

It's a funny thing—the English language. *Business* is a bad word in some quarters, but *businesslike* is all right. *Management,* to some, means manipulation, or at any rate controlling, and is therefore something to be shunned, yet we like things to be manageable and even well-managed. *Organizations* can put people off, but no one wants to be disorganized.

It is not the words, however, that let us down, it is the institutions. To be truthful, we have not always run our institutions as if people mattered. We call our buildings and our machines our assets, while our people are our costs. We have treated people as "hands" or as "labor" or, not much better, as "human resources." We have seen the job of a manager as planning, deciding, implementing, controlling—doing things *to* people rather than *with* them or *for* them. But the mood is changing.

This is an optimistic book because I remain convinced that human beings are endlessly capable of surprising us and themselves, that everyone can do better and can do more, that trust and openness are cheaper and more effective than checks and controls.

There will be disappointments. There are people whose only concern is for themselves. There are bullies and braggarts who seek to make things happen by shouting and by fear. There are cheats and scoundrels, there are people who wilt under responsibility and others who run away from challenges.

"It is not for sale," I said to the developer.

He persisted. The offer for my house was three times what it was worth. He was going to turn the surrounding area into a building site anyway. I capitulated. I asked the lawyers to draw up a contract. I set about planning to move. It became exciting. I, and my whole family, got involved. We signed a contract for another house. The day before we were meant to exchange contracts on my house the developer rang. There was a snag. His financial backers were away. Could we delay things a bit? It went on like that, for a week, then a month. Eventually I confronted him.

"You're not going to buy it, are you?"

"No, I guess not," he said, "not at that price."

"I played fair with you," I said, "I trusted you. I made huge commitments because of you and you never had any intention of paying that sort of money. I'm never going to trust anyone like you again."

He looked at me. "Have you lived so long and only just learned that lesson?" he said.

"Most people I meet are not like you," I replied.

"You'd be surprised," he said.

We must not let such people set our standards for us. I still believe, in spite of many disappointments, that the great majority of people prefer to be trusted and not distrusted, would like to have great things expected of them rather than be assumed incompetent, would enjoy encouragement more than reprimands and would, after a bit of eye-blinking disbelief, respond enthusiastically to anyone who treated them like that. Even the bullies and the braggarts are often shy cowards underneath; they know no other way. You get back what you give out.

Organizations, however, are confusing places. We can easily forget the simple lessons. "I have ever hated all nations, professions and communities, and all my love is towards people," said the poet Alexander Pope. He then went on, "but principally I hate and detest that animal called man, although I heartily love John, Peter, Thomas, and so forth." I agree as long as he adds a Mary, and a Catherine, and a Kate, to the John, Peter, and Thomas. Organizations today no longer talk about their "hands" or even, much, of their "human resources." They are, have to be, built around individuals. We each now have to stand behind our own name tag.

I am happy about that. This book is about how to get the most out of named individuals. That, today, is the real secret to getting organized. It is also very exciting, watching people start to blossom and organizations begin to hum.

> "I know the theory," she said, irritably, "but putting it into practice is quite another thing. You are no better," she went on, "you don't practice half of what you preach."

She had a point. To understand is not enough; one must also make it happen. If youth, as they say, had the wisdom of age, or age the energy of youth, the world would be a better place.

I know, from my own experience, that the ideas in these chapters are true for most of the people I meet for most of the time. These ideas do work, allowing for the odd freak, criminal, or madman. To use them, however, to go beyond understanding and into action, requires, often, a degree of courage (to go against convention), a lot of trust (that people will behave as you expect them to), and considerable patience (because the world turns slowly and people do not change their colors or their behavior overnight).

I have, myself, however, a list of ten excuses for not practicing what I preach:

I don't have the time.
The job can't wait.
They are not up to it.
They would not understand.
I cannot trust them.
It's my job so I must do it.
Sticks make people jump, carrots don't.
They prefer being told what to do.
Let's face it, I can do it better myself.
They've got too much on their plate.

They are all excuses. Without courage, trust, and patience, whatever understanding or whatever theory we may have counts for nothing. This book, therefore, like all books, has its limitations. Ideas it can give you, but never courage, nor the willingness to trust others, nor the patience to wait for others to grow into that trust, nor the patience to forgive. In the end, getting organized means making no excuses for not treating people properly. It is really very simple, but very difficult.

Index

A

Academics, 123, 132, 162
Accountants, 38
Accounting, 141–148
Achievement markers, 14, 16
Achievement motivation, 12–17, 21–22, 131, 133, 178
Administrative organizations, 121
Administrator, team role of, 100, 101
Adult role, 81–89
Advice-giving, 85
AIDS laboratory, effects of internal competition in, 60–61
Alchemy humors, 7
All I Really Need to Know I Learned in Kindergarten (Fulghum), 84–85
Alliance building, 95
Allied Dunbar, 14
Apollo people, 127, 129–131, 133; identifying, 133–139
Apollo syndrome, 99
Appearances, 107–114. *See also* Impressions; Signs
Appreciation of investment, 142–143
Ardrey, Robert, 29
Arts, 124
Assets, appreciating versus depreciating, 142–143
Assumptions, appearances and, 107–114
Athena people, 127, 131–132, 133; identifying, 133–139
Attribution theory, 67–69
Authority, 90, 93; earned, 92–93; outward and visible signs of, 111
Awareness, 87–88; of parent-adult-child games, 87–88; territorial, 33–34

B

Bay of Pigs invasion, 104
Bechtel, 60
Belbin, M., 99–100

Berne, E., 82, 83, 88
Bible, 41
Blanchard, K., 76
Bloomingdales, 60
Boards, 104
Bodyguards, 111
Borneo, 5, 9
"Bottom drawer it" tactic, 95
Boundary setting, 41
Brainstorming, 84
Brass rubbings, 148
Breakeven point, 145
Bribery, 16
British Airways, 110
British driving test, 59
British school examinations, 59
British stereotype, 44
British teams, 98–99
Bullies and braggarts, 183
Businessmen, 150
"But in the future..." tactic, 96

C

Calculation, psychological contracts based on, 22
Campbell-Walker, F., 57
Captains, 100–101
Careers: changing nature of, 176–182; role suitability and, 52–53
Carers, 23–24
Cash flow, 147, 148
Cash versus profit, 146–147
Catalysts, outsider, 104–105
Caught, avoidance of being, 75, 76
Chairperson, 99, 102
Change: in nature of work, 176–182; unsuitability of Apollo managers for, 129–131; unsuitability of role tribe for, 120–121
Charity work, 182
Cheats and scoundrels, 112–113, 183–184
Child role, 81–89; encouraging creativity and, 84–85
Children: achievement markers for, 16; curiosity of, 160; parenting, 86; territorial security of, 32
Chinese agents, trading agreements with, 25
Chinese box of jobs, 53–54
Choleric humor, 7
Clients. *See* Customers
Clothes, 47, 111–112
Club tribe, 117–119; communication in, 117–118; organizational idea of, 117; people in, 119; picture of, 117, 118; situations appropriate to, 118–119
Clubhouse, office space as, 181
Coaches, 105
Coercion, psychological contracts based on, 22
Comfort-clinging, 87
Commitment, 125, 172
Committees, 101–102; teams versus, 101–102
Common knowledge, in Johari Window, 45–46, 48
Communication: in club tribe, 117–118, 119; outward signs and, 113; in role tribe, 120; as top problem, 33–34
Communication skills, 3
Company Worker, 100
Competition, 58–64; benefits of, 59–60; destructive, 60–61, 62; external, 61–62; internal, 60–61; marathon versus horse race, 58–64; pricing and, 145, 168;

questions for thinking and talking about, 63–64
Compliments. *See* Praise; Stroking
Compromise: committees and, 101–102; power politics and, 95, 96, 97
Conflict: destructive competition as, 60–61; territorial, 30–31
Construction, 124
Consultancies, 122, 124, 131
Consultants, paying, 175
Contracts: job, 37; marriage, 19–20; psychological, 19–26; two-way nature of, 24–25
Contractual fringe, 169–170; management of, 172; paying, 175
Control: in large, traditional organizations, 167–168; over job duties, 36–42; power and, 90; of results versus process, 172; in shamrock organizations, 172–173
Conventions, 46
Cooperation, psychological contracts based on, 22
Core responsibilities, 37, 38–39; specification of, 41
Core workforce, 169; management of, 173; reduction of, 179
Corinthians, 158
Costing, 141–148
Costs: investments versus, 141–143; pricing and, 144–145, 148, 168; questions for thinking and talking about, 147–148; real versus opportunity, 145–146; variable versus fixed, 143–144
Counting, 141–148
Coward, Noel, 11
Creative child, 84–85
Credit, taking or giving, 35, 67–68
Cricket, 98
Criterion referencing, 59
Criticism: self-concept and, 71, 72; stroking and, 74–76
Crosby, P., 151
Cuba, 104
Curiosity: brakes on, 163; habit of, 159, 160; learning and, 158–166
Customers, 149–157; as everywhere, 152–154; finding, versus jobs, 157; as first priority, 154–156; as forever, 150–151; as inconvenient, 154–155; internal, 153–154; as purpose of business, 149–150; questions for thinking and talking about, 156; and shamrock organization, 174; strategic planning based on, 155–156; zero defects and, 150–151

D

De Charme, 6
Deflection, 96
Deming, W. E., 150
Departments: as internal customers, 153; tribes and, 116
Depreciation, 142–143
Deviousness, 76
Diary, 179
Differences, 1–9; within businesses, 4; within families, 4; in humors, 7; individual, 1–9; in intelligence types, 1–5, 9; in management styles, 126–127; obvious, 6; between organizations, 115–117; between origins and pawns, 6; questions for thinking and talking about, 8; recognizing, 6–8;

within schools, 4; within society, 4; stereotyping and, 3–4; teams as collections of, 99–101, 106; between Type A and Type B people, 6–7; uniting, into common cause, 4–5
Digital, 60
Dionysus people, 127, 132–133; identifying, 133–139
Directing, 90
Disabling Professions (Illich), 87
Dissonance reduction, 69–70
Divisions, tribes and, 116
Doctors, 123, 132
"Doctors and patients" game, 87
Dress, 47, 111–112
Driver, team role of, 100, 101
Dyaks, 5, 9

E

"E" factors, 10–18; lack of, 10–11; listed, 10; money versus other motivators for, 11–17; questions for thinking and talking about, 17
Economics, 141–148, 174
Effervescence, as "E" factor, 10. *See also* "E" factors
Efficiency: office design and, 110; standardization and, 28
Effort, as "E" factor, 10. *See also* "E" factors
Electrician job, 36, 40–41
Emotional tactic, 96
Empowerment, inside-out donut and, 36–42
Empty space, of inside-out donut, 39–41
Energy: competition and, 59, 60; as "E" factor, 10. *See also* "E" factors
Enthusiasm, as "E" factor, 10. *See also* "E" factors
Examples, 73
Excitement, as "E" factor, 10. *See also* "E" factors
Executives: competition for jobs of, 61–62; marriage patterns of, 22–24; retired, as consultants, 124
Expectations: attribution and, 67–69; high, 65–66, 67; image gap and, 66–71; inside-out donut view of, 36–42; role, 54–55; secret contracts and, 19–26; self-fulfilling prophecy and, 65–73; teacher, 65–66
Expenditure, as "E" factor, 10. *See also* "E" factors
Expert power, 91, 92–93, 95
Expert(s): contracting out, 169–170; customers and, 155; learning versus relying on, 158–159; team role of, 100, 101
External competition, 61–62

F

Faculty, 123–124
Failing, fear of, 62
False clues, 112–113
Families: cash flow of, 147; coercive contracts within, 22; Greek gods and styles of, 133; individual differences within, 3–4; tribes and, 115
Family businesses, 104
Feedback: characteristics of helpful, 71; stroking and, 74–80

Finisher, team role of, 100
First impressions: organizational, 107–109; personal, 43–45
Fixed costs, 143–144
Flattened organizations: inside-out donuts in, 40; negative power and, 94; top jobs in, 62
Flexible labor force, 170–171; changing nature of work and, 176–182; growth in, 171; management of, 172–173, 181
Flexible work agreements, 30
Flexi-lives, 176–182; defined, 179
Fluor, 60
Football, 178
Forgiveness, 48, 163–164
Forming stage, 102, 103
France, school schedule in, 38–39
Friedman, 6–7
Fulghum, R., 84–85
"Further investigation is required" tactic, 96

G

Games, 81–89; "doctors and patients," 87; healthy, 84–85; "If it weren't for him," 83–84; parent-adult-child, 82–89; questions for thinking and talking about, 88; sales, 83; "Why does this always happen to me?" (WAHM), 84
Games People Play (Berne), 82, 83, 88
Generals, 104
Genuineness, 79
German railway, 78
Glory ladder, 14
Goal setting, psychological contracts and, 24–25
Gods, Greek, 100, 126–140; Apollo, 129–131, 133; Athena, 131–132, 133; Dionysus, 132–133; families and, 133; management styles and, 126–127; names of, listed, 127; questionnaire for identifying, 133–139; tribes and, 127; Zeus, 127–129, 133
Golf handicap, 62–63
Government treasuries, 147
Governments, as closed teams, 104
Grading, 59
Greeks, ancient, 2; gods of, 100, 126–140
Groups: Athena people and, 131–132, 133; language and culture of, 32; task tribe and, 121–122; territorial markers, 31–32. *See also* Teams
Groupthink, 104–105
Growth stages of teams, 102–104

H

Harmony, Apollo people and, 129–131
Harrision, R., 55–56
Harvard University, 2
Hazing, 69–70
Health authority staffing, 175
Hewlett-Packard, 60
Home-school partnerships, 24
Horizontal fast track, 52
Horse races: internal competition as, 61; marathons versus, 58–64; questions for thinking and talking about, 63–64
Hospitals, customers of, 152
Human needs, 10–18
Humors, alchemist, 7

I

Ideals, 72
Identity: jobs and, 50; roles and, 51–57
Idiosyncrasies, 140
Idleness, 10–11
"If it weren't for him" game, 83–84
Illich, I., 87
Illness, inventing, 87
Image gap, 66–71; attribution and, 67–69; dissonance reduction and, 69–70
Impressions: first, 43–45, 107–109; Johari Window and, 43–50; organizational, 107–114; outward and visible signs and, 107–114
In Search of Excellence (Peters and Waterman), 60, 63–64
Influence, 90–91, 93; power politics and, 94–96
Information: as resource power, 95; as territorial marker, 31
Inside-out donut, 36–42; core responsibilities in, 37, 38–39, 41; defining boundaries of, 41; expanded responsibilities in, 39–41; picture of, 37; questions for thinking and talking about, 42
Intellectual property, 143, 173
Intelligence types, 1–5, 9
Internal competition, 60–61
Internal customers, 153–154
IBM, 14, 60
Interpersonal intelligence, 3
Intrapersonal intelligence, 3
Investments: costs versus, 141–143; people as, 143
Invisible man tactic, 96
"Involved" people, 22–24
Iranian revolution, 97
Irish clover, 168. *See also* Shamrock

J

Jackson, L., 65
Japan: customer satisfaction in, 150; empowerment in, 40; horizontal fast track in, 52
Job boxes, in role tribe, 119–120
Job descriptions, 37, 129–131
Job enlargement, 40
Job responsibilities: core, 37, 38–39, 41; defining boundaries of, 41; expanded, 39–41; inside-out donut view of, 36–42
Job territories, 29–31
Jobs: changing nature of work and, 176–182; Chinese box of, 53–54; competition for top, 61–62; finding customers versus, 157; identity and, 50; role suitability and, 52–54; role web and, 54–56
Johari Window (house), 43–50; common knowledge (Room 1) of, 45–46, 48; origins of, 45; picture of, 45; private room (Room 4) of, 45, 46, 47–48; public room (Room 2) of, 45, 47, 48; questions for thinking and talking about, 49; rooms of, defined, 45; unconscious room (Room 3) of, 45, 48–49
Johnson & Johnson, 60
Journalists, 162, 180
Juran, J., 150

K

Kanter, R. M., 60–61, 64
Kennedy, J. F., 104

L

Labor exploitation, 171
Large organizations, 167–168
Learners, characteristics of good, 164
Learning, 158–166; blockages to, 162–163; encouraging, in organization s, 165; forgiveness and, 163–164; implicit theories of, 159; incomplete process of, 161–162; questions for thinking and talking about, 165; relying on experts versus, 158–159; selfishness and, 164; sponge theory of, 159; *they* syndrome and, 162–163; wheel of, 159–166. *See also* Wheel of learning
Life: flexi-, 176–182; what people want from, 14–15; work portfolio and, 177, 178
Life list, 64
Line managers, devices used by, to fend off unpopular recommendations, 95–96
Logical intelligence, 2, 3
London Marathon, 58
Loners, 22–24
Lost opportunity, 145–146
Love, 47–48
Loyalty, 125, 172
Luxuries, 15

M

Maccoby, M., 127
Malaysia, 163, 166
Management: of contractual fringe, 172; of flexible workforce, 172–173, 181; Greek gods and, 126–140; of people with large donuts, 41; of shamrock organizations, 172–174; styles of, 126–149
Management by Objectives, partnership in, 24–25
Management-by-walking-about, 54–55
Managers: Apollo style of, 129–131, 133; Athena style of, 131–132, 133; as customers, 153; devices used by, to fend off unpopular recommendations, 95–96; Dionysus people and, 132–133; open-house style of, 31; person tribes and, 123–124; resistance of, to shamrock organization, 173–174; satisfaction factors of, 62; task tribes and, 122; Zeus style of, 127–129, 133
Manipulation, 79
Marathons: external competition as, 61–62; horse races versus, 58–64; questions for thinking and talking about, 63–64
Marginal cost pricing, 144–145, 148
Markers, achievement, 14, 16
Market niche, 154
Marketplace, discipline of, 145
Marriage: basis of lasting, 106; patterns of executives', 22–24; psychological contracts in, 19–20, 22–24; tribes and, 115
Marx, Karl, 26
Mastermind learning, 164
Melancholic humor, 7
Mentors, 86–87, 89
Mikado, The, 53
"Mobilizing political support" tactic, 95
Money: cash versus profit, 146–147; counting and costing

of, 141–148; "E" factors and, 12–17; for necessities, 12, 15–16; other motives versus, 12–17, 21–22, 178; questions for thinking and talking about, 147–148. *See also* Costs
Monitor Evaluator, 100
Monopolies, 145, 150, 168
Mothers, 53, 85, 179–180
Motivators and motivation: "E" factors and, 10–18; monetary versus nonmonetary, 11–14, 21–22, 178; stroking as, 74–80
Museums, customers of, 155
Music band, 103–104
Musical intelligence, 2

N

Natives, asking the, 9
Necessitities, money and, 12, 15–16
Needs, human, 10–18
Negative power, 91, 93–94, 95–96
Net, task tribe, 121–122
Nitty-gritty tactic, 95
Norm referencing, 59
Norming stage, 102, 103

O

Objectives, job, 37
Objectives setting, psychological contracts and, 24–25
Occasional workers, 170–171, 172–173
Office space: as daytime home, 180–181; efficiency and, 110; as outward and visible sign, 107–114; predicting individual characteristics based on, 27–29; predicting organizational culture based on, 108–109; private territory and, 27–29, 31–32, 34, 180–181
Office-sickness, 110
Oil company, 167–168, 177
Olympic spirit, 62
One-Minute Manager (Blanchard), 76
Open house, 31
Openness: Johari Window approach to, 43–50; of teams, 104–105
Open-plan office, 31
Opportunity costs, 145–146
Organizational chart, in role tribe, 119–121
Organizational idea(s): of club tribe, 117; concept of, 117; of role tribe, 120; of task tribe, 121
Organizational structure, shamrock. *See* Shamrock
Organizations: categories of, 115–125; customers within, 153–154; differences and generalities among, 115–117; encouragement of learning in, 165; large, 167–168; named individuals in, 184–185; outward and visible signs of, 107–114; shamrock, 167–175; small, 104, 118–119; tribes and, 115–125
Origins (personality type), 6
Outputs monitoring, 172
Outsourcing, 169–170
Ownership, of rules, 77–79

P

Parent role, 81–89; restraining, 85–86
Parent-adult-child (PAC), 82–89
Parents as customers, 152, 153

Parties, 84
Partnerships: Dionysus people in, 133; as person tribes, 123–124; psychological contracts in, 23–25
Part-time workers, 170–171, 172–173
Patrick, St., 168
Paul, St., 158
Pawns, 6
Payslips, 26
People: Apollo managers and, 129–130, 133; Athenian, 131–132, 133; in club tribe, 119; as cost versus investment, 143; Dionysus, 132–133; importance of, 183–186; in person tribe, 123–124; in role tribe, 121; in shamrock organizations, 169–174; in task tribe, 121–122; Zeus managers and, 128–129, 133
Performance appraisals, 125; attribution and, 68–69; openness versus privacy in, 47
Performing stage, 102, 103
Person tribe, 123–124; organizational idea of, 123; people in, 123–124; picture of, 123
Personalities: in club tribes, 118–119; Zeus people as, 127–129
Persuasion, 93
Peters, T., 60, 63–64
Pettigrew, Andrew, 95–96
Phlegmatic humor, 7
Physical intelligence, 2
Physical space: efficiency and, 110; as outward and visible sign, 107–114; predicting individual characteristics based on, 27–29; predicting organizational culture based on, 108–109; private territory and, 27–29, 31–32, 34, 180–181; types of, 180–181
Plant, team role of, 100
Playpens, 84
Policemen, 111
Policing, 75; self-enforcing rules versus, 77–79
Polite society, 46
Politics, 60, 90, 94–96
Pooh-Bah, 53
Pope, A., 184
Portfolio careers, 176–182
Position power, 91, 92, 93, 95; abuse of, 95–96; Apollo people and, 129–131
Power, 90–97; of Apollo managers, 129, 133; of Athena people, 132, 133; of Dionysus people, 132–133; expert, 91, 92–93, 95; language for, 90–91; negative, 91, 93–94, 95–96; politics and, 90, 94–96; position, 91, 92, 93, 95–96; questions for thinking and talking about, 96–97; resource, 91, 93, 95; territory as, 33; types of, defined, 91; of Zeus people, 128–129, 133
Practical intelligence, 2, 3
Practices, 123–124
Praise, 70, 74–80
Predictability: Apollo managers and, 129–131, 133; role tribe and, 120–121
Pricing, 141–142; above cost versus below price, 144–145, 168; psychology of, 148
Priests, 111
Private self: false signs and,

112–113; in Johari Window, 45, 46, 47–48
Prizes, 58–59
Problem sniffer, 161
Problem solving: Athena people for, 131–132; learning and, 164; task tribes for, 122
Problem solving ability, 3
Procter & Gamble, 60
Professionals: Dionysus people as, 132–133; in person tribes, 123–124; in portfolio careers, 180; in shamrock organizations, 173
Professors, 123, 132, 162
Profit: cash versus, 146–147; importance of customers versus, 149
Promotion, territorial security and, 33
Psychoanalysis, 48–49
Psychological contracts, 19–26; of calculation, 22; of coercion, 22; of cooperation, 22; expectations and, 19–26; misperceiving, 20–22; questions for thinking and talking about, 25–26
Public self: false signs and, 112–113; in Johari Window, 45, 47, 48
Pubs, 108
Punishment, 74–76
Purchasing manager, 172
Purpose, competition and, 59–60

Q

Quality: for customer retention, 150–151; zero defects approach to, 42, 78–79, 150–151
Questioning culture, task tribe as, 122
Questionnaire for identifying gods, 133–139
Questions stage of learning, 160

R

Real versus opportunity costs, 145–146
Reception areas, 109
Recommendations, fending off unpopular, 95–96
Recruitment, in club tribes, 119
Reflection stage of learning, 161
Rejection tactic, 95
Religions, 124
Reorganization, redistribution of territory in, 32–33, 181
Representatives, committee, 101–102
Reprimands, 74–76
Resource Investigator, 100
Resource power, 91, 93, 95
Responsibility: learning and, 162–163; parent-adult roles and, 85–86
Rituals, 46
Role Negotiation exercise, 55–56
Role occupants, 48, 121
Role tribe, 119–121; communication in, 120; organizational idea of, 120; people in, 121; picture of, 119–120; situations appropriate for, 120–121
Role web, 54–56
Roles, 51–57; age and, 52; choosing appropriate, 52–57; importance of, 51–52; interpretation of, 56; negotiation of, 55–56; in organi-

zations, 53–57; parent-adult-child, 82–89; questions for thinking and talking about, 56–57; self versus others' perception of, 54–55; team, 99–101
Rosenbaum, 6–7
Rosenthal, R., 65
Routine work: Apollo managers and, 129–131; Athena people and, 131; role tribe and, 120–121
Rowing eight, 99
Rules, 76–79; Apollo managers and, 129, 133; negative power and, 96; ownership of, 77–79; in role tribes, 121; self-enforcing, 77–79

S

Safe, playing it, 62
Sales competitions, 61
Sales game, 83
Sanguine humor, 7
Sarawak, 5, 9
Sarcasm, 75
Scapegoat tactic, 96
Schedules, 38–39, 78, 179
School prize day, 58–59
Schools and schooling: closed teams in, 104; customers of, 152, 154; intelligence types and, 3; learning versus, 158–159, 164; norm versus criterion referencing in, 59; praise versus reprimands in, 75–76; programming in, 39; shamrock organization for, 171; teacher expectations and, 65–66
Screens, privacy, 46
Season tickets, 143–144
Secret contracts, 19–26
Security: stroking and, 76; territory and, 32–33
Selection: in club tribes, 119; Zeus managers and, 128–129
Self: Johari Window view of, 43–50; parent-adult-child model of, 81–89; roles and, 51–57
Self-concept: attribution and, 67–69; bashing, 71; boosting, 70–71; dissonance reduction and, 69–70; expectations and, 65–73; image gap and, 66–71; power of, 71; truth and, 71
Self-employed, flexible workforce and, 171, 180
Self-enforcing rules, 77–79
Self-fulfilling prophecy, 65–71; expectations and, 65–73; image gap and, 66–71; positive uses of, 70–71; questions for thinking and talking about, 72
Selfishness, learning and, 164
Service recipients, as customers, 152–153
Shamrock, 167–175; contractual fringe in, 169–170, 172; core workforce in, 169, 173; elements of, 169; flexible labor force in, 170–171, 172–173; management of, 172–174; origins of, 168; questions for thinking and talking about, 174; resistance to, 173–174
Shaper, 99
Shouting, 74–75
Signs, outward and visible, 107–114; assumptions and, 107–114; deliberately misleading, 112–113; individual, 27–29,

110–111; organizational, 107–114; questions for thinking and talking about, 113–114
Small organizations, 104, 118–119
Spatial intelligence, 2, 3
Specialist recommendations, political games regarding, 95–96
Spider web, 117–119
Sponge theory, 159
Sports, 124
Sports teams, 98–99, 100
Standardization, self-expression and, 28
Standards and standard-setting: attribution and, 67–69; competition and, 59; examples as, 73; for zero defects, 42, 78–79, 150–151
Stars, in person tribes, 123–124
Stereotypes and stereotyping, 3–4, 44, 110–111
Storming stage, 102, 103–104
Stroking, 74–80; genuine, 79; power of, 75–76; questions for thinking and talking about, 79; reprimands versus, 74–76; rules and, 76–78; standards and, 78–79
Stupidity, assumption of, 159
Succession, 61–62
Supermarket checkout clerks, 16, 39–40
Suppliers, standards for, 151

T

T group, 43–44
Talents, parable of the, 41
Targets, job, 37
Task tribe, 121–122; organizational idea of, 121; people in, 121–122; picture of, 121, 122; situations appropriate for, 122
Teachers: contracting, 171; expectations of, 65–66; praise versus reprimands from, 75–76; self-enforcing rule use by, 77
Team Worker, 100
Teams, 98–106; Athena people and, 131–132; basis of, 106; closed versus open, 104–105; as collections of differences, 99–101, 106; versus committees, 101–102; groupthink in, 104–105; growth stages of, 102–104; key points about, 99; outsiders as catalysts for, 104–105; questions for thinking and talking about, 105–106; roles in, 99–101; in shamrock organizations, 173; sports, 98–99, 100; task tribe and, 121–122. *See also* Groups
Teenagers, 47, 92
Telecommuting, 181
Telepathy, 113, 117
Telephone style, 109
Television credits, 35
Temporary workers, 170–171, 172–173
Tenure, 123
Territorial Imperative, The (Ardrey), 29
Territory, personal, 27–35; awareness of, 33–34; disputes over, 30–31; of groups, 31–32; job, 29–31; physical, 27–29, 31–32, 34, 180–181; protecting, ways of, 31–32; psychological, 29–34;

questions for thinking and talking about, 34; reorganization and redistribution of, 32–33, 180–181; self-expression and, 27–28; shared, 181
Tests stage of learning, 160–161
TI, 60
Theories stage of learning, 160
They syndrome, 162–163
3M, 60
Thriving on Chaos (Peters), 63–64
Thrusters, 22–24
Thyssen, Baron, 57
Ticket scalper, 150
Timetables, 38–39, 78, 129
Toyota, 170
Trade unions, and shamrock organization, 174
Training group, 43–44
Training programs, 70, 87
Transactional analysis (TA), 82–89
Tribes, 115–125; club, 117–119; Greek gods and, 127; mixes of, in organizations, 115–117, 124; names of, listed, 117; person, 123–124; questions for thinking and talking about, 125; role, 119–121; task, 121–122
Trust, 166, 183–184, 185; Zeus people and, 128–129
Truth, self-concept and, 71
Type A personality, 6–7
Type B personality, 6–7

U

Uganda kob, 29, 31
Ulysses, 127, 131
Unconditional positive regard, 47–48
Unconscious: games as, 82; in Johari Window, 45, 48–49
Uniforms, 46, 111–112
University management, 123

V

Variable costs, 143–144
Victim, 83–84
Videotaping, of team processes, 105
Volunteer work, 182
Volvo, 79

W

Wages, fees versus, 26
Warrior goddess, 127, 131–132
Waterman, R., 60
Watson, T., 14
Wheel of learning, 159–166; brakes to, 162–163; forgiveness and, 163–164; picture of, 159; questions stage of, 160; reflection stage of, 161; shortcuts or blockages in, 161–162; tests stage of, 160–161; theories stage of, 160
When Giants Learn to Dance (Kanter), 60–61, 64
"Why does this always happen to me?" (WAHM) game, 84
Win-win versus win-lose orientation, 58–64
Work: in bits and pieces, 176–182; changing nature of, 176–182; "E" factors in, 10–18; marathon versus horse race approach to, 58–64; what people want from, 13–14
Work design, in role tribes, 121
Work portfolios, 176–182
Work satisfaction factors, 13–15,

21, 62; work portfolios and, 178–179
Workforce: contractual, 169–170, 172; core, 169, 173; flexible, 170–171, 172–173, 176–182

Z

Zero defects, 42, 78–79, 150–151
Zeus people, 127–129, 133; identifying, 133–139